Groups Within Organizations

Peter B. Smith

Groups Within Organizations

Applications of Social Psychology to Organizational Behaviour

Harper & Row, Publishers
London New York Evanston San Francisco

First published 1973

Published by Harper & Row Ltd
28 Tavistock Street London WC2E 7PN

Standard Book Number 06-318008-0 (cloth)
Standard Book Number 06-318009-8 (paper)

Printed by Richard Clay (The Chaucer Press), Ltd, Bungay, Suffolk

Contents

Index of Figures and Tables

To Frances, Alison and Ruth

Preface

This book has two principal origins. The first of these is my experience in teaching social psychology to successive generations of undergraduates. Each year I have found myself faced with cogent, well-argued incredulity that laboratory experiments in social psychology tell us much about what goes on within real-world organizations. Each year I have been forced to re-think and elaborate the reasons why I believe that laboratory experiments do have some relevance, provided that they are interpreted in a manner which takes account of the differences as well as the similarities between laboratory experiments and real organizations.

The second spur to my writing has arisen more from my own reading of research into social interaction in groups. I have become increasingly impatient with many of the distinctions which are traditionally made. For example, 'conformity', 'attitude change', 'leadership' and 'interpersonal attraction' are all concepts frequently used to describe social influence processes in groups. Yet the distinction between these concepts as separate processes has nowhere been tested by research, and their retention appears to have more to do with convention than it does with the findings of research. In this book I attempt to show that it is more fruitful to think in terms of just two social influence processes: social comparison and control. I have attempted to show how these concepts can be used to tie together existing research and to illuminate the implications of that research for the study of organizations. A consequence of this is that the book reads most coherently if read sequentially: the later discussion rests on the treatment of social influence processes in the opening chapters.

I should like to acknowledge the permission of the McGraw-Hill Book Company to reproduce Figure 1, page 11; *Personnel Psychology* to reproduce Figure 2, page 41; the American Psychological Association to reproduce Figure 7, page 52; and the Harvard Business School to reproduce Table 1, page 65.

The imperfections of this book must remain my own responsibility, but I should like to express gratitude to a number of people who helped it into being. John Child and Paul Kuipers found me a somewhat reluctant author, but they persevered and finally persuaded me to go ahead. John Child, Cary Cooper, Eve Godfrey, Tony Manstead, Roy Payne, Diana Pheysey, John Southgate, Frances Smith, Michael Willson and Karl Weick made valuable comments on an earlier draft. Angela Pead and Sue Calver typed the manuscript.

PETER B. SMITH
Brighton, July 1972

I Introduction

This book is concerned with the ways in which we influence one another's behaviour. What it has to say arises out of research conducted by investigators over the past thirty or forty years. The research has been detailed, laborious and often confusing, and we have not yet reached the point where clear, unifying principles have emerged. It may perhaps be useful to start by trying to compress what is to be said into a couple of paragraphs, to provide a brief overview.

In analysing the ways in which we influence one another, social scientists have found it useful to distinguish between small face-to-face groups and the often larger organizations which are so characteristic of our society. An *organization* is a social system explicitly set up to influence its members towards the achievement of some goal. A *group*, on the other hand, may arise in a variety of ways, but it is defined by the existence of continuing face-to-face relationships between its members. Group members very frequently influence one another also. In recent years the analysis of organizational behaviour has grown somewhat apart from the study of social influence in groups. But it is important to inter-relate the two fields because organizations are for the most part made up of overlapping systems of innumerable small groups. This book will attempt to build some bridges between these two fields.

The varieties of social influence to be found within organizations are probably rather few. This book is organized around the proposition that there are in fact just two processes of social influence, which we will call social comparison and control. Social comparison occurs in any situation in which one uses another person as a reference point in determining one's own actions. This might be when one is uncertain of oneself. Alternatively, it might be in a situation in which one's relationship to another person leads one to wish to behave in the same way as that person, or indeed in the opposite way. In each of these instances a process of *social comparison* occurs. This process is explored in detail in

Chapter II. A second form of influence occurs where some other person imposes demands on one to behave in a particular way. Such a person might be an appointed leader, but equally he might be someone with no defined *right* to give orders, who none the less sets out to influence one. This second process will be termed the process of *control.*

Before reviewing the remaining chapters of the book, it is worth pausing to consider whether there are any particular reasons why it might be useful to look at influence as two processes rather than one or three or some other number. A great many studies, some of which we shall explore presently, have concluded that there are two principal dimensions of behaviour in groups. For example, such conclusions have emerged from the study of leaders' behaviour, ratings of small group discussions and studies of parent–child interaction. Danziger (1971) has suggested why this might be. He points out that social influence processes almost always involve just two parties. At some points in this book we shall refer to them as 'Person' and 'Other'. Even when we come to look at more complex forms of organizational influence, there are still often two parties to the influence process, even though many individuals are concerned. If there are just two parties to the process of influence, then clearly there are two possible modes of influence. Firstly, Person may voluntarily choose to relate his behaviour to that of Other; secondly, Person may respond to some kind of deliberate pressure from Other to behave in a particular way. These two possible modes of influence correspond to the processes which are here termed social comparison and control.

When the two central processes of influence have been explored in Chapters II and III, the next three chapters examine a number of constraints and limitations on the application of the concepts to different settings. In Chapter IV the characteristics of the physical environment are examined. The manner in which the environment modifies or limits social influence processes is considered. The ability of a group or organization to function effectively will reflect the degree to which it has achieved a balance between the processes of influence within it and the environment in which it functions. Chapter V is devoted to an analysis of this proposition as applied to small groups. The effectiveness of organizations is dependent not only on those processes operating within groups but also on relations between different groups. Groups, like individuals, make social comparisons with one another and make control demands on one another. These processes are outlined in Chapter VI. The nature of the influence occurring within groups and organizations is bounded by time constraints. Where interaction is known to be finite certain advantages accrue, which may be used in stimulating flexibility and change. Chapter VII discusses group-training procedures which take off from this point of departure. Membership in temporary groups can often fail to generate change in long-term organizations from which the temporary groups derive. The problem of instituting change within organizations, or organizational development as it is often called, is the concern of the final chapter.

One of the most pressing problems facing the social sciences at present is the gulf between understanding a phenomenon and being able to change it. In chemistry, if one understands the properties of a certain compound it is a relatively simple task to use that knowledge to transform it into something else. But if one understands the reasons why conflict occurs between two groups, this does not necessarily make it any easier to affect the outcome of that conflict. To intervene in a situation effectively may require quite different skills from those required to understand it. This is partly true also in the physical sciences; one needs not only knowledge of the properties of particular compounds but also the practical skills of carrying through a particular experiment. But in chemistry it is the theoretical problems which are difficult and the practical skills are relatively easily acquired. In the social sciences the theoretical models are not so difficult to grasp, but the implementation of change is a major problem. There are a number of differences between the physical and social sciences which account for this.

Perhaps the two most important differences are the degree of control the physical scientist has over his materials and the durability of the properties of a given product in the physical sciences. The chemist is able to control the purity of his materials, the conditions under which they react and the duration of the reaction to a very considerable degree. The social scientist is never in this position. The people whose behaviour he is studying show infinitely greater variability and the conditions under which they interact are only partially controllable. Different people perceive a situation which is objectively identical in differing ways, thereby nullifying the social scientist's attempt to standardize a situation. He may explain the purpose of his study using identical words to many people. But one person will attend to what he says, while a second will take more account of the ease or anxiety with which he says it. A third will fail to hear the explanation at all while being preoccupied with some other concern, but a fourth person who is suspicious will scan his every word for signs of the devious intentions of the researcher.

A second important difference between the physical sciences and the social sciences is what Homans (1967) has termed the 'historicity' of social science. In other words people's behaviour is affected by their previous experience. A group will respond to a controlling autocratic leader differently depending on whether that is what they are accustomed to, or whether they are more used to a leader who shares decision-making with his group (e.g. Lippitt and White, 1958). In contrast, the reactions studied by the physical scientists are more easily replicable. Oxygen gas atoms behave in the same manner, no matter whether they have previously been a part of a sugar molecule, or of water, or of caustic soda. In brief, people remember some of what happens to them, thereby making each separate experience distinctive.

This book will lay emphasis in the early chapters on understanding the behaviour observed to occur within groups and organizations. Later there will be more emphasis on methods of attempting to implement change. This sequence reflects the manner in which this field of study has developed. A series of studies which first gave an indication of what it was that needed understanding were the celebrated 'Hawthorne' studies. These were conducted at the Hawthorne works of the Western Electric Company in Chicago in the late 1920s (Roethlisberger and Dickson, 1939). In the first study (the 'Relay Assembly Test Room'), various changes were made in the working conditions of a group of five girls. It was found that no matter what was the nature of the changes introduced, the girls' productivity rose. This was true even after the fourteenth change, which was the elimination of all the benefits previously introduced and the restoration of the status quo. The fact that the girls' productivity continued to rise is a clear demonstration of the 'historicity' of their reactions. The investigators concluded that the changes in productivity were due to the fact that the experimenters had sought the advice of the girls at each stage as to which changes to introduce next. By expressing interest in the girls they had modified the situation in an unintended manner. In a second study (the 'Bank Wiring Observation Room') a group of fourteen men worked at wiring up telephone banks for nearly nine months, while under constant observation. No changes were deliberately introduced. The investigators were particularly interested by the very steady level of productivity the men showed. They concluded that the level was well below what the men could have done, and that the level was held where it was by a variety of social influences within the work group. They noted the manner in which those who wired up around 6,600 connections per day were accorded approval and favours by the others. Those who worked harder than this attempted to conceal the fact and those who worked below the norm were shown various forms of disapproval by the group.

The Hawthorne studies made an impact out of all proportion to their conclusiveness. The Relay Assembly Test Room data in particular is suspect since it was based on only five girls and two of these were changed in mid-experiment. With the passage of time and the accumulation of data from other situations it becomes easy to see that some of the findings were specific to the place and time of the study. Carey (1967) questions whether the studies proved much at all. In many ways, what the studies proved is no longer important; what they certainly did was to provide a focus for the growth of interest in the study of group and organizational behaviour. The Hawthorne studies constituted a first, crude, attempt to apply scientific method to the analysis of behaviour within organizations. In the first study an experimental approach was adopted and in the second a more naturalistic, observational approach. In the Hawthorne studies, the observational approach proved the more fruitful. It yielded a rich harvest of information, which could be used to construct hypotheses about group behaviour. An influential book, *The Human Group,* was published by Homans in 1950, which used the Bank Wiring Observation Room data in precisely this manner.

In order to test these hypotheses about groups, one needs increasingly to make use of experimental methods. Observation is best suited to the development of descriptions of what happens in a group; but experiments are best suited to determining what causes the observed events. For instance, if the Bank Wiring study were repeated in a number of different factories (see, e.g., Lupton, 1963) we should be in a position to assert how widespread restrictive productivity norms are. But we should not be able to say anything very much about what causes restrictive productivity norms to develop. The development of studies of groups over the past thirty years has been very much in the direction of experimental methods. Researchers have tried to get closer and closer to the methods used by the physical scientists. They have taken it as established that social influence processes are very frequent in the groups and organizations that comprise society and have attempted to create similar processes within controlled laboratory settings.

An early attempt to use experimental methods was that of Lippitt and White (1958). Using real youth clubs, they attempted to compare the effect of three different styles of leadership behaviour. The clubs were composed of eleven-year-old boys and the leaders were adults, briefed to play a different leadership role with each club. Each club experienced the various leadership styles in succession, while each leader played a different role in each club. The experiment is in many ways impressive. It yielded the findings that the 'democratic' leadership style was superior on a number of criteria to the 'autocratic' and 'laissez-faire' styles. However, the autocratic style led the children to produce the greatest number of models. The experiment shows how an experimental change in a group can be seen to cause a measurable effect. But it is difficult to be sure quite what it was about the way the experiment was staged that led to the findings coming out as they did. Of course, they might come out that way under any circumstances, but it is equally possible that any one of a number of other factors could have contributed to the effect. For example:

(1) The experiment was staged in the late 1930s, a time when there was world-wide concern about totalitarian systems of government.
(2) The experiment took place in the United States, a country in which considerable value is often attached to participative forms of decision-making.
(3) The subjects of the experiment were children, while the leaders were adult; while this is characteristic of some leadership processes in our society, it is uncharacteristic of others.
(4) The researchers' account of their work leaves one in little doubt that they personally favoured the democratic leadership style. It is quite possible that they role-played this style in a more convincing manner than the other two styles.

One might argue that these are finicking criticisms, which achieve no more than a blurring of the original clarity of the experiment. Researchers in the field would reply that it is only through attending to such uncontrolled (and uncontrollable) variation between one experiment and the next that we can achieve any certainty that the effects we are studying are of general applicability rather than being very specific to the setting we are studying.

The Lippitt and White experiment is relatively naturalistic, in so far as it used real youth clubs. Most recent experiments use settings which are much more radically simplified. For example, experiments on the determinants of bargaining behaviour (Gergen, 1969) typically use a format where two players bargain with one another and each has only to choose between two alternative courses of action. In many experiments even the second player is dispensed with: the experimental subject is led to believe that he is bargaining with someone else, but in reality the messages he receives are predetermined by the experimenter. In this manner the experimenter can explore what responses he gets to a variety of co-operative or competitive strategies, which would never be possible if he studied only settings where both bargainers were real.

The trend in studying social influence is thus towards creating ever more simplified, but highly controlled, experimental settings. It is easy to argue that such settings are 'artificial' and that what goes on in them will have little relevance to behaviour in more 'natural' groups or organizations. This criticism needs to be examined carefully, since the majority of research findings to be presented in this book derive from just such 'artificial' settings.

The artificiality of the laboratory experiment in social psychology derives from several sources. Perhaps the most important of these are that participants in laboratory experiments are usually strangers to one another, the experiments do not usually last long, and the participants are rather frequently students. Let us examine these points in turn.

At the beginning of this chapter it was argued that a group could be defined by the existence of continuing relationships between its members. In terms of this definition, many laboratory experiments are not studies of groups at all. Golembiewski (1962) suggests that we should describe them instead as 'collectivities' to point up the contrast between meetings of initial strangers and meetings of a number of people with interpersonal relationships already established. Plainly there are differences between long-established groups and experimental collectivities. The question is whether these differences will impair our ability to understand one by studying the other. Weick (1967) has suggested what some of these differences may be. He argues that a participant in an experiment is rather like someone on his first day in a job:

> A person who is in an experiment is like the newcomer on the job, often has low confidence in his judgements, is easily influenced, misunderstands instructions, is uninformed, finds the job novel and interesting, is cautious, and tolerates many demands that would anger him in more familiar settings. Many of these behaviours dissipate as he becomes more accustomed to the assignment.

This indicates that in collectivities, members are rather more likely to go along with what they think the other members or the experimenter wants them to do. Thus if we wish to use such experiments to assess *how much* social influence occurs in groups we shall certainly be misled. For example, the experiments of Asch (1956) are often quoted to illustrate conformity behaviour. In these experiments participants were pressured into misperceiving the length of lines by accomplices of the experimenter who deliberately gave incorrect responses. This kind of experiment clearly tells us nothing about the incidence of conformity in other settings. But if what we want to investigate is what *causes* people to go along with the judgements of others under certain circumstances, it is as good a setting as any other in which to study this.

The viewpoint that groups are 'natural' while collectivities are 'artificial' should be resisted. We shall be examining in Chapter IV the manner in which the environment constrains the formation of any group or organization. Neither a group nor an organization can usefully be thought of in a vacuum; its form and structure arise out of an interplay between people and their environment. Indeed, groups frequently arise from what are initially collectivities. Newcomb (1961) has plotted the manner in which relationships developed over a year in a collectivity of seventeen students at the University of Michigan. The students were offered free accommodation in a house in exchange for agreeing to be the subjects of Newcomb's research. 'Natural' groups probably arise rather frequently from such environmental proximity.

The second aspect of laboratory experiments to be discussed is their short duration. If experiments are short, then we should expect that most participants will not be greatly concerned about what happens in them. Their long-term relationships should be more important to them. The simplest way to minimize involvement is to do what is expected of one and pass on to something more motivating. This line of reasoning is supported by Hovland (1959). He reports that while experimenters frequently obtain marked attitude changes in one-third to one-half of their experimental subjects, those engaged in field studies of the effects of the mass media report much lower incidences of change. More recent research since the advent of television does not indicate any modification of this conclusion (Weiss, 1969). Hovland's view is that the short-term experiment focuses attention on a specific message provided by a high prestige experimenter on a subject about which one does not care too much. In response to the mass media on the other hand, people have been shown to be selective, ignoring, distorting, forgetting or switching off messages with which they disagree. At least some of these messages are about topics which are important to them. Thus short-term laboratory experiments will provide a poor guide to the *amount* of opinion change to be expected in society; but they provide a setting in which people do attend to messages they receive. As such they are a very good setting for studying what factors do sometimes cause people to change their opinions.

Another much criticized aspect of laboratory experiments is that they are very frequently conducted with students as subjects. The reasons for this are usually that they are much more readily available than anyone else. Since students differ considerably from the general population in terms of age, social class, intelligence and salient motivations, it is difficult to defend this state of affairs. There has been a slight trend in recent years towards the use of a broader range of subjects. One of the most notable points concerning the use of students is that students are part of the same organization as the experimenter. In American universities students of psychology are often required to participate in a certain number of experiments, and in any university students will be aware that there is an ill-defined link between the experimenter and those who assess his standing in the university. These qualities of experiments with students indicate that one should indeed be cautious about generalizing from a series of experiments unless at least some of them have been conducted with alternative populations.

Argyris (1968) has described a number of similarities between the subject in a psychological experiment and the shop-floor worker in a factory. He points out that in both situations people are given very precise instructions as to what they should do, but they are not told why. In fact in both settings the authority figure is so concerned to conceal his goals that he engages in a certain amount of deceit. This may be in the form of lying, but more often it takes the form of leaving unsaid things which if spelled out would reveal too much. Thus in both settings participants are subjected to arbitrary control, requiring them to perform tasks with little apparent meaning. Argyris is critical of this state of affairs for reasons we shall consider shortly; let us first consider the advantages of this convergence. The exercise of arbitrary control is characteristic not only of the industrial shop-floor but also of all the major organizations of our society: schools, hospitals, social work agencies, universities and firms. Control is usually more arbitrary at junior levels and more reasoned at senior levels, but even at senior levels concealment is widespread. Argyris (1969) has reported data from a wide range of meetings of senior management supporting this viewpoint. If this behaviour is so widespread, its occurrence in the laboratory experiment is an asset rather than a handicap. It indicates that what goes on in experiments is likely to parallel (perhaps in heightened form) what happens in organizations. Rather than exclude this from the experiment, it should be assessed and included in analyses of why the results were obtained.

One might argue, as does Argyris (1968), that concealment is unnatural and that if one studies groups of friends or T-groups (described in Chapter VII) one finds instead a pattern of openness, trust and risk-taking. Such groups are equally worthy of study and are to be found within as well as outside organizations. But it does not seem likely that it will help much to label one type of group as more natural than the other. Most probably the difference is the difference between the type of group structure which emerges where power differences are high and where they are low. Argyris's viewpoint has something in common with the viewpoint of some Marxists, who argue that in describing groups and organizations as they are in our society, one implies that it is impossible to structure society in any other way and is thereby an instrument in the preservation of the status quo. The viewpoint of this book is that any potential changes in our society should indeed arise out of an extended examination of how things are currently. Such an examination can provide us with some concepts with which to assess and predict the likelihood of success of various kinds of innovation. Accordingly, the first six chapters of this book are almost entirely given over to studies of groups and organizations as they currently are. In the final two chapters the focus is turned to an analysis of some aspects of innovation and change, which draw on the concepts developed earlier.

It is time to return to the basic theme of this book, the relation between group behaviour and organizational behaviour. We have characterized a group as a number of people having continuing face-to-face relationships, and an organization as a social system explicitly set up in order to influence its members towards goal achievement. Clearly there is potential overlap between these definitions. A farmer with half a dozen employees or a tailor with an assistant would constitute both groups and organizations. But as a system increases in size it rapidly becomes impossible for everyone to be in face-to-face contact with everyone else. Even among the fourteen men in the Bank Wiring Observation Room there was some evidence of a split into two cliques, one sitting near the front of the room and the other near the back. In Chapters II and III evidence will be presented detailing the powerful influence which groups have on their members. The much larger organization cannot guarantee being able to influence its members so forcefully. To be sure the groups which comprise the organization will influence *their* members, but the influence of the group may be in a direction quite different from that intended by the organization. This was illustrated by the Bank Wiring study: the group standards tended to hold down rather than enhance productivity.

The Bank Wiring study illustrates a situation where the group's goals were in conflict with those of the organization. One should avoid the conclusion that such conflicts occur only between shop-floor groups and management. Dalton (1959) has documented numerous instances of conflict between managerial groups and their organizations. Such conflicts will often but not always occur. They can clearly be either severe or less so. Likert (1961) has outlined a theory of organizational behaviour in which he argues that the system of overlapping group memberships which make up a large organization constitute the major channel of influence within the organization. A manager's role, in Likert's view, is that of acting as a 'linking pin' between the various groups to which he belongs. In some of these groups he will have

FIGURE I *Likert's linking pin model of an organization**

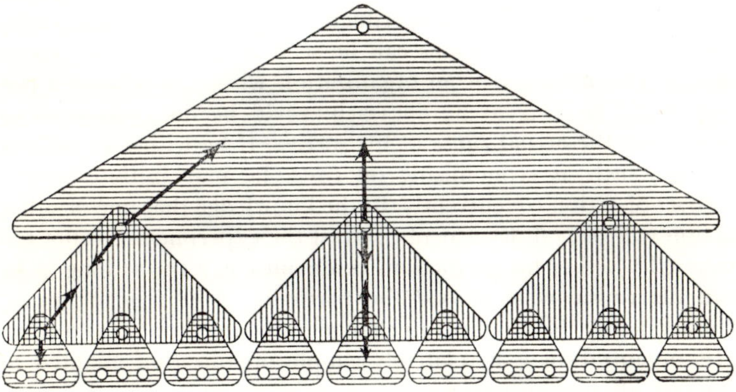

(The arrows indicate the linking pin function)

* Taken from *New Patterns of Management* by R. Likert. Copyright 1961 R. Likert. Used with permission of McGraw-Hill Book Company.

high power, if he is the organizational superior, other groups will be groups of colleagues, and in still others he will be a subordinate. Figure 1 shows a picture of an organization conceived in this manner. The task of the occupant of a given role would be to ensure that the demands of the various groups on one another are communicated and decided upon. The ease or difficulty of doing this will depend on the nature of the different groups and the tasks they are engaged upon.

Groups, then, often but not always arise as sub-units of large organizations. How does this affect our earlier discussion of the laboratory experiment? Experiments are a form of temporary organization: they are set up to influence participants to behave in ways which will prove or disprove hypotheses. Relationships are not typically all face-to-face: the organization also includes research assistants and directors whom the subjects themselves will meet only at the end or even not at all. The experimental collectivity is a much better simulation of a fragment of a large organization than it is of a face-to-face group relatively autonomous from its environment. Perhaps its greatest similarity is to a transaction between an organizational fragment and its customers. As with other organizations, a good deal of what occurs may be a consequence of the real or imagined wishes of the high-power figures within the system, in this case the experimenter. Researchers have recently become very conscious of the need to minimize the degree to which experimenters unwittingly give their subjects cues as to what response they are hoping for. If they do give such cues, their theories may be spuriously verified (Rosenthal and Rosnow, 1969).

In the same way that experiments can be seen as temporary organizations, organizations can be seen as uncontrolled experiments. The manager of an organization wishes to achieve a certain goal: so long as he does achieve it, he does not need to determine the actual *cause* of his success. If he wishes to make a change, such as economizing on costs, he may initiate several courses of action concurrently, in the knowledge that one or other action will pay off. By way of contrast the experimenter is not too worried whether his predictions come out correctly, so long as he can determine what *caused* the particular results he obtained. Consequently, he attempts to change only one variable at a time. His organization is a relatively simple organization adapted to the task of answering why.

Whether or not we can make use of the findings of experimental studies turns out to depend on the nature of social influence processes at work in different settings. The findings will be most useful in settings, such as are found in many organizations, where people are cautious, uninvolved and puzzled. They will be less useful in settings where people are secure and highly motivated.

In view of the differences between experiments and organizations, a certain amount of sober caution is necessary in interpreting either experiments *or* organizational case studies. In the chapters which follow we shall attempt to place side by side experiments and organizational studies. Where both types of study yield analogous findings, we may be much more confident about their validity, since the strength of one method is the weakness of the other.

Summary

The goal-oriented systems which we call organizations are made up of numerous overlapping face-to-face groups. The complexity of the interplay between the individual's response to the various groups to which he belongs and to the organization as a whole comprises the subject-matter of this book. Case studies of organizations in the field provide rich descriptive material, whose strength lies in the recording of the frequency and complexity of phenomena which occur. Experimental studies of groups on the other hand provide a much simplified picture, better adapted to the answering of questions as to what causes what. The 'historicity' of human behaviour means that answers derived from short-term experimental groups cannot automatically be assumed relevant to field settings. A careful comparison must be undertaken of convergences and divergences between experimental and field findings.

This book advances the hypothesis that social influence processes in both groups and organizations can be analysed under two headings: social comparison and social control. The hypothesis is developed from small group studies and later applied to organizational studies.

II Social Comparison Processes

Let us begin by considering a series of laboratory experiments which illustrate both the strengths and the weaknesses of experiments outlined in the last chapter. A girl arrives at a psychology laboratory to participate in an experiment. She is met by someone who introduces himself as Dr Grigor Zilstein saying that he is researching into the effects of electric shock. She is led into a room, which has in it a large machine. Some measurements are made and then she is told that it will be necessary to wait for ten minutes while the machine is adjusted in various ways. Some of the girls are told that the shocks they are to receive are very mild, while others are told that they will be quite painful though not dangerous. Each girl is than told that some people prefer to wait by themselves, while others prefer to wait in company. A choice is then made between the alternatives and the girl proceeds to the appropriate waiting-room. Ostensibly the experiment has not yet begun, but actually it is finished. No shocks were administered and all that remained to be done was to ask the girls to complete some questionnaires and to explain to them why they had been misled.

Schachter and his co-workers, who conducted this research, were interested in what they called the psychology of affiliation. Their prediction was that when the girls were more anxious, they would prefer to be with others. Schachter (1959) reports that this is indeed what they found: when the shock was described as 'quite painful' sixty-three per cent preferred company, compared with thirty-three per cent in the 'very mild' condition. Such a difference would arise by chance alone less than one time in a hundred. What caused the girls to behave in this way?

Schachter considers five possible explanations. It is possible that the girls felt they wanted to escape from the situation: getting together with others could provide opportunities for discovering how to get out of the experiment. Alternatively they may have felt confused and anticipated that being with others would help to clarify what was going on. A third possibility was that the girls were anxious and that being with others would help to reduce the anxiety. Anxiety might be reduced by direct communication with the others, or by some kind of distraction. Finally, the girls may have found themselves uncertain what they felt about the novel situation: on this explanation their motive for being with others would be to find out how others were reacting to the situation.

An ingenious series of modifications to the experiment was used to eliminate some of these possibilities. It was found that the effect was only obtained if the people with whom the girls were given the opportunity of waiting were also waiting for the same experiment. On the other hand it made no difference whether they were permitted to talk to one another or not. Evidently what the girls favoured was a situation where they were with others who shared their fate, but with whom verbal communication was not essential. This effectively rules out the escape hypothesis, the clarification hypothesis and the distraction hypothesis. The first two of these would need some conversation and the last would be best served by waiting with others unconnected with the experiment. This leaves two possible explanations – direct anxiety reduction and comparing oneself with others.

Some of Schachter's studies included various measures of how much anxiety the girls felt. In a further experiment by one of Schachter's team (Wrightsman, 1960) the girls actually did complete a five-minute waiting period. Wrightsman's measures showed that waiting with others did not actually reduce anxiety more than waiting alone did. Furthermore he showed that if one examined the anxiety scores of a particular set of girls who waited together, their scores tended to converge on a mean figure. This did not happen if one arbitrarily grouped together the scores of those who waited alone. In short, what these studies show is a process of social influence. The influence is rather unlike what one might at first call to mind if one considers social influence as a process. One might visualize social pressures and argument, whereas in this experiment the influence occurred without even a single verbal communication taking place. Where verbal communication *was* permitted influence still occurred but its form was more complex. Among groups who could talk and who had a narrow range of anxiety levels, social influence was found; but where the range of anxiety levels was initially wide, it tended to stay that way.

It is time to start examining the significance of these experiments. They are contrived and short-term and based on a situation quite unlike everyday life for most of us, but we should not let this distract us from their undoubted value. They create a situation in which the girls feel uncertain of themselves and then test theories which try to account for how the girls respond. Situations in which people in groups and organizations feel uncertain of themselves are exceedingly widespread, and it is for this reason that the studies are of interest. Schachter's view is that when situations are ambiguous or uninterpretable in terms of past experience, we seek social validation for our responses. Put more bluntly, he is saying that we do not know what we feel about novel events until we see how others react to those events. This constitutes a rather radical view of human experience. The traditional view would emphasize the link between the experience of anxiety and measurable physiological events, like levels of adrenaline in the blood: one feels anxious if an experience elicits high blood adrenaline. Schachter's view turns the causal chain around: one experiences anxiety and high blood adrenaline if others appear to be alarmed. A girl in the early part of the experiment might think something like, 'This all feels strange and unfamiliar – I'm not sure how to react.' One subject is quoted in Schachter's book as saying, 'I wanted to wait with other people to see how they would react while waiting for the experiment. By seeing that they weren't worried then I wouldn't be.' Such a quotation obviously does not establish that that is how all the girls thought, but it does put Schachter's theory in somewhat more concrete terms.

One of the bases on which Schachter's work rests is Festinger's (1954) exposition of social comparison theory. While Schachter was concerned with emotions and especially with anxiety, Festinger's discussion is far more wide-ranging. Festinger postulates that we each have a drive to evaluate our opinions and abilities. Given the choice we prefer objective, non-social means of evaluating ourselves. Thus we prefer to verify our ability to drive a car or our opinion that it will rain tomorrow by objective test rather than by finding someone who says we can drive well or agrees that it will rain tomorrow. But often objective non-social criteria for evaluating ourselves are not available and under these conditions we use social criteria. Festinger argues that we tend to use as comparison objects people who are similar to ourselves: this enables a more accurate assessment of where we stand. Schachter's research fits neatly into this: his experiment did not provide non-social means for self-evaluation, and his girls did choose to compare themselves with others in the same experiment rather than more dissimilar people.

The formulation of Festinger's model poses a number of questions which will be with us for the remainder of this chapter. One might ask first of all, how frequently is it the case that people do not have available objective, non-social criteria for self-evaluation? Secondly, where such criteria are unavailable, it is important to examine how people select whom they shall compare themselves with. Is Festinger right in claiming that one always selects someone as similar to oneself as possible? Thirdly, and perhaps most importantly, what are the consequences of such comparisons? In Schachter's work the consequences were increased consensus within each group as to how much anxiety was in order. More generally, the consequences of social comparison are sometimes likely to be what social psychologists call conformity behaviour. But the term conformity is so loaded with pejorative value in everyday speech that it may be more fruitful to analyse separately the various forms of social influence that may arise out of social comparison.

How widespread is ambiguity?

The first issue to be examined is how widespread are objective non-social criteria for self-evaluation. It is easiest to think of such criteria in the instance of abilities. Sportsmen, craftsmen and the technically skilled all have the possibility of comparing their performance against fairly objective yardsticks. Opinions are only testable in this way where they take the form of predictions about the occurrence of future events. One's own feelings are the least easy of all to test against non-social criteria. From this discussion one might anticipate finding a rather wide range of bases of social comparison. For instance a group of skilled shop-floor workers might base their self-evaluations on evidence available to them about their expertise in successfully accomplishing skilled tasks. On the other hand a group of middle managers within an organization have very poor criteria for judging their effectiveness. They are much more likely to make use of social criteria.

This difference in the bases available to different groups is intensified if one considers how they spend their time. For the skilled shop-floor worker, the primary task is non-social. He may spend a fair amount of his time talking to others, but this is not intrinsic to his job. He may interact with others or avoid them, as he wishes. The manager's task on the other hand lies in interacting with others. For example, Horne and Lupton (1965) in a study of sixty-six British managers found that they spent two-thirds of their time talking with others. Most of the time was given over to transmitting information to others or to explaining.

These data were collected by asking the managers and their secretaries to keep records over a sample week. Other studies (e.g. Carlson, 1951) found that senior executives spend an even higher proportion of their time talking to others.

The managers of any type of organization are faced with some ambiguity about its effectiveness, and hence with some ambiguity about their own effectiveness. This is perhaps least true in a small one-product manufacturing organization, where there is some chance of relating decisions to their consequences. With increased size of the organization this will less and less often be the case. Likewise within other organizations, such as schools, hospitals or universities, objective feedback to the management will be hard to come by. Some years ago a survey was conducted in the United States by R. L. Kahn and associates (1964) at the University of Michigan. The survey was designed to provide an estimate of the incidence of role conflict and role ambiguity in the working population. Interviews were conducted with 725 people who were working for pay at the time. They comprised a representative sample of the U.S. workforce. The questions in the survey emphasized social rather than non-social sources of information. It emerged that almost all the respondents would like more information than they currently had. The survey concentrated more on those who were so deprived of information that this caused them some distress. Kahn *et al.* report that:

35 per cent were disturbed by lack of clarity about the scope and responsibilities of their job.
32 per cent were under tension because they were uncertain about their superior's evaluation of them.
31 per cent were disturbed by lack of information about opportunities for advancement in the organization.
29 per cent were bothered by ambiguity about what their co-workers expected of them.

Kahn *et al.* do not subdivide their figures for the incidence of ambiguity by status levels within their sample. They do, however, report a strong association between reported ambiguity and a measure of tension. Tension is shown to be much higher in managerial and professional groups than among operatives and unskilled workers.

So far it has been argued that social comparison processes will operate most powerfully where non-social bases for comparison are unavailable. The data reviewed suggest that most people feel a need for a clearer basis for social comparison than they get. This is particularly so at managerial levels in organizations. It is also likely to be the case within short-term laboratory experiments, since here one is confronted with a novel situation and very little feedback on one's performance.

Choosing a comparison object

The second major question to be explored concerning social comparison processes is that of how one chooses a comparison person. Festinger's proposition is that we choose someone similar to ourselves. This should enable us to obtain the most clear and accurate information from the other. Schachter-type experiments can be used to enhance our understanding of what types of similarity or difference are most important. The original Schachter experiments leave us unclear whether the girls were choosing to be with other girls because they were girls or because they were also in the experiment. In a later study, Darley and Aronson (1966) arranged for three girls at a time to arrive for the shock experiment. Of each trio, two of the girls were actually confederates of the experimenter. After the purpose of the experiment had been explained the girls were asked to rate how nervous they felt. One of the confederates in the experiment always chose a point on the scale one point above that chosen by the true subject. The other confederate always chose a point two points below. The experimenter then gave the true subject the choice of waiting alone or with either of the other two girls. The results showed that she usually chose to wait with the girl one point *more* nervous than herself. This suggests in accordance with Festinger's theory that it is similarity of experience which is important, since although the girl was more nervous she was also the most similar. Of course by choosing someone more nervous than herself as a comparison object, the girl may also have found some consolation.

A number of other laboratory experiments have been reported which use a somewhat different format. Groups of six to eight subjects are asked to complete a task or test which purports to measure some aspect of their personality or abilities. The experimenter then indicates to the subjects the rank order of scores which the different subjects have obtained. He states that the design of the research permits him to share with each subject the exact score of one of the other subjects. The subject then chooses which score from the range he would like to see. Social comparison theory would of course predict that one would choose the rank nearest to one's own. Wheeler *et al.* (1969) showed that where the attribute being measured was a desirable one, subjects chose the next rank up the scale. Where the attribute was an undesirable one, they chose the next rank down. Subjects were also more likely to choose comparison persons above themselves where they were more highly motivated (Wheeler, 1966). Thornton and Arrowood (1966) indicated to their subjects that there was an unexpected discontinuity in the range of scores. Where their scores fell at the point of discontinuity, it was found that subjects chose to compare themselves to the person on the other side of that discontinuity, rather than the more similar person within the same subgroup of scores as themselves. Hakmiller (1966) gave his subjects two tests. On the first test, they were led to believe that they had scored relatively low on 'hostility to one's parents'. On the second test the subject found he had scored more towards the high end of the scale. Under these conditions subjects did not choose to compare themselves with those who were most similar but with those who had achieved the most hostile score of all.

These findings suggest that social comparison may serve a variety of functions. Under different circumstances one might wish to compare oneself with someone who was worse than oneself, about the same, or considerably better. Festinger's model turns out to be oversimple on this point. Which type of comparison person one chooses will clearly depend on the purpose of the comparison. Schachter's subjects were afraid and uncertain and chose someone like themselves; Wheeler's (1966) subjects were motivated to improve their performance and chose those one or two places above themselves; Hakmiller's subjects were threatened by unpleasant feedback and chose someone far below them.

We have now reviewed another series of laboratory experiments. The findings arise from relatively few studies, but they present a rather coherent picture. What is missing so far is any data indicating how people choose comparison persons in more naturalistic settings. As soon as one starts to think about this problem the differences between experimental and naturalistic settings crop up once more. Within the experiment, the researcher makes sure that the subject compares himself with someone, and indeed with only one of the possible available comparison persons. Outside the laboratory, no such certain situation is to be found. If someone is a member of a particular group, it need not follow that he compares himself with the members of that group. For example, studies of industrial workers who do not adhere to restrictive productivity norms (Collins, Dalton and Roy, 1946) indicate that they frequently come from very different ethnic, religious or educational backgrounds. They may belong to a particular work-group on the basis that management have assigned them to that particular group, but they do not share the values, identifications or criteria for hard work which govern their colleagues' behaviour.

The writer Thoreau, who argued that 'the social deviate is in reality but dancing to a more distant piper', conveyed the essence of the hypothesis that we all respond to a comparison person or comparison group somewhere. The difficulty with this way of formulating the social comparison model is that it becomes all too easy to analyse any set of findings on a *post hoc* basis, as showing that a particular person identifies with some group to whom his behaviour appears related. For example, the classic studies of the *American Soldier* during the Second World War (Stouffer *et al.*, 1949) generated much data showing comparative levels of satisfaction in different units. Non-combatant troops stationed in Europe were found to be much more satisfied than those remaining in the United States, despite the far superior conditions in which the troops in the U.S. were to be found. This finding was 'explained' by postulating that the troops in Europe compared themselves with troops on active service, who were in far more deprived circumstances, while the troops at home compared their conditions with those of civilian life. The explanation is plausible, but no data are available as to whether the troops did in fact make the comparisons postulated.

In the field the process of social comparison is intertwined with that of social attraction. This is illustrated by two studies by Newcomb. In the first of these (1943), the effect of three years' attendance at Bennington College, a liberal arts college, were studied. Those students whose values became more liberal in accordance with the dominant campus climate identified with others who were liberal. Those who did not move from their initial conservatism were more closely identified with their predominantly conservative families. From the data we cannot say whether those who changed did so because they were attracted to others on campus, or alternatively whether leaving home led them to select comparison models on campus, who in time became attractive. Newcomb's later study (1961) is more specific and therefore valuable to this analysis. Newcomb offered seventeen students free accommodation in a house for a semester at the University of Michigan. During the semester, he made repeated measurement of the development of interpersonal attraction among the seventeen. He found that his data increasingly approximated a 'balance' model, whereby A likes B if B likes the same things which A likes. This was particularly true in the instance of perceived attraction to oneself. In other words A is most likely to like B where he perceives that B likes A. Newcomb's analysis is not phrased in terms of social comparison, but he makes use of a related concept, 'consensual validation'. Each student is seeking to validate his perceptions by finding those who will verify them. Newcomb's data illustrate a situation in which Festinger's postulate that comparison persons will be similar to ourselves is upheld.

While similarity and attraction may often provide the basis for comparison processes, it will be recalled that some of the laboratory experiments showed that this need not always be the case. In situations of threat and competition the comparison persons were more dissimilar. Comparisons concerning the equity of wage differentials and wage negotiations in general provide instances of such situations in the field. In the fight for equal pay for women, women negotiators select as comparison persons men doing the same work for more pay, while those resisting them implicitly argue that women should compare themselves with women in other jobs. The choice of comparison person is thus crucial to one's position.

Patchen (1961a, b) has studied the selection of comparison persons by workers in a refinery. In line with the argument advanced in this chapter, Patchen rejects the notion that one always compares oneself with the most similar person. In evaluating one's abilities in comparison with others it is plausible to expect that one aspires towards being satisfied with the outcome. But, suggests Patchen, in the instance of wage comparisons there may be circumstances in which one *wants* to be dissatisfied. This could arise in the situation where one is underpaid but blames this fact on others rather than oneself. It is not easy to argue that if one's *ability* turns out low in relation to the comparison person it is someone else's fault. But if one is underpaid, it is rather easy to blame the management rather than see it as a valid assessment of one's worth. In these circumstances one may prefer to compare one's wages with someone who gets a better bargain than oneself. Selecting such a comparison will serve to legitimize discontent and hence bargaining for an improved wage.

Patchen interviewed 519 workers in a Canadian oil-refinery. He asked them to name two other employees who earned different amounts from themselves. The interviewees were then asked to say how they felt about the differentials involved and why. Patchen categorized the comparisons as 'dissonant' comparisons and 'consonant' comparisons. Dissonant comparisons were those where there was a poor match between the relative wages and the relative attributes required to do the job, such as age, seniority, skill, experience, etc. In consonant comparisons there was a good match. Patchen's finding was that those most likely to make dissonant comparisons were those who were both poorly paid themselves and also believed that advancement was not a consequence of personal effort and initiative. Those who were better paid or who did believe that effort and initiative were rewarded were more likely to choose consonant comparisons.

These findings cast a rather different light on the process of social comparison. The studies we have examined earlier such as Schachter's or those deriving from Festinger's theory portray the individual as someone in search of feedback from his environment as to what he is like or what he should do. Patchen's subjects, who differed from the others in that they were outside the psychology laboratory, sound much more sure of themselves. For them the function of social comparison is not so much the reduction of ambiguity but rather the maintenance of an existing set of beliefs about one's worth as a person. The ways in which social comparison can achieve this are best illustrated by examination of the consequences of such comparisons, to which we therefore now turn.

The consequences of social comparison

A good deal of research has been conducted into this issue. We shall first review some rather general models of the consequences and then turn to some more specific analyses of the effects of wage equity and inequity.

The consequences of social comparison are clearly going to depend on what the comparison shows. There are three possible classes of situation, which may be termed ambiguity reduction, confirmation and disconfirmation. *Ambiguity reduction* will occur in Schachter-type settings where the person making the comparison is faced with a novel situation and is uncertain what to do. In the Wrightsman (1960) experiment, which derived from the Schachter design, what actually happened is that the anxiety scores of the group members converged on one another, at least where there was not too wide a range of anxiety scores. Another illustration of this effect is the studies of Sherif (1936) into the 'autokinetic' effect. Subjects sat in a totally dark room and were asked to estimate the movement of a point source of light. The light did not in fact move at all, but it was found that subjects were strongly influenced by one another's estimates, until after a time consensus would emerge in the group. Behaviour in panic and disasters (Schultz, 1964) is similar. In all these situations ambiguity is high, so one follows the lead of one's comparison person. This phenomenon has been termed 'informational' social influence. It is difficult to make any kind of estimate of its prevalence.

If social comparison leads to *confirmation* by the comparison person, one might initially think that there would be no particular consequences to predict from this event. The subject sees himself a certain way and he discovers that someone else sees him the same way. This would be to leave out of account the motivating properties of the confirmation experience. If another confirms one's self-evaluation, one is likely to like him the better for it. The Newcomb study (1961) showed how attraction and confirmation are interwoven. Increased liking may in turn lead one to utilize the other as a comparison person on a broader range of issues. One may question whether confirmation of poor self-evaluation would have quite these consequences, but the evidence on this point is sparse. Deutsch and Solomon (1959) found that subjects who felt that they had performed poorly did not distinguish between other subjects who told them they had done well and other subjects who told them they had done poorly. They liked each about equally. The effects of confirmation are much understudied, but the suggestion is that, paradoxical though it is, confirmation may generate change.

Psychologists have devoted by far the most resources to the third possible outcome of social comparison, namely *disconfirmation*. If I evaluate myself or some aspect of my behaviour or opinions favourably and my comparison person does not, I am faced with what has usually been termed imbalance (Heider, 1958) or dissonance (Festinger, 1957). Festinger's definition of dissonance is that it exists where one holds two cognitions, one of which is psychologically the obverse of the other. Thus if I perceive myself to be a good tutor and ask my students for comments on the course I have just taught them, when they tell me that I have failed in many respects I experience dissonance. Critics of dissonance theory (Brown, 1965) have been quick to point out that one cannot infer whether or not dissonance is present unless one knows more about the context of the two cognitions. In the example just cited, for me to experience dissonance I must also perceive my students favourably; if I see them as untrustworthy or idle, their feedback will not generate dissonance for me.

Festinger postulates that dissonance is an uncomfortable state which one seeks to reduce. There are a number of ways in which this is possible. Among those available to me would be:

changing my opinion of my teaching abilities;
seeking information from other students;

seeking information from other tutors, as to what the same students said to them;
forgetting or misunderstanding what they said;
changing my opinion of the students.

Some of these models of dissonance reduction would be more probable than others because by using them I would create greater or lesser amounts of dissonance with other cognitions I have.

Festinger's model of man is therefore one of someone striving to maintain the consonance of his cognitions in the face of periodic disconfirmations. A great many laboratory experiments have been completed which seek to test various aspects of dissonance theory (Aronson, 1969). Here we shall only be concerned with those studies showing that when faced with disconfirmation from a number of experimental subjects on a judgement task, one tends to yield towards the majority verdict. This happens not only in situations where ambiguity is high but also in situations where one would have no difficulty in making a correct judgement in the absence of others. The best known of these experiments was conducted by Asch (1956), who used judgements of the length of different lines as his experimental task. Related work, for example by Crutchfield (1955), has shown that similar effects can be obtained when subjects are asked to assess the truth or falsehood of opinions on topics such as the correct population of the United States.

Thus one manner in which one can reduce the dissonance engendered by the discovery that others see the world differently from oneself is by conforming to the judgement of the others. Some people may do this on the basis of expediency, while others may really believe that the others are more correct in their judgements. The experimental designs employed have usually permitted the subjects only to conform or to remain independent, but there are further possibilities which are likely to be equally important in the field. Hollander and Willis (1967) have argued that conformity behaviour should be analysed along two separate dimensions, which they term dependence–independence and conformity–anticonformity. We can examine these dimensions within the framework of the social comparison model which has been used in this chapter.

Dependence–independence refers to the degree to which the subject uses the other as a comparison person. Someone may make very discrepant judgements, but if I am not using him as a comparison person my behaviour will be unaffected by him. On the other hand the more strongly I compare myself with particular others, the more I become open to their influence. In Chapter I, the Bank Wiring group was reviewed, which showed a high level of mutual dependence. A study by Seashore (1954) of 229 industrial workgroups in the U.S. showed that in the more cohesive groups there was more uniformity of output than in the less cohesive groups. The cohesive group might be either highly productive or highly unproductive, depending on other factors, but in either case it was more uniform than the non-cohesive group.

Conformity–anticonformity refers to the manner in which the subject responds to disconfirmation from his comparison other. If he conforms, his behaviour moves towards that of his comparison other; if he anticonforms his behaviour moves away from his comparison other. Either form of movement is a form of dependence. Experimental studies of anticonformity are rare, but this reflects the interests of researchers in the field rather than the lack of significance of the phenomenon. Willis and Hollander (1964) have experimentally demonstrated the separability of conformity, anticonformity and independence. In field settings it is often the case that by conforming to the judgement of one comparison other, the subject anticonforms to that of another comparison other. For example in the Bank Wiring group productivity conformed to the group standard, but it anticonformed to management's expectation.

Research into conformity has been bedevilled by implicit value judgements made by the researcher. Most usually the researcher disapproves of conformity and approves of independence. This writer's prejudices are somewhat different; to me it appears that each of the three possible modes of response – conformity, anticonformity or independence – have both strengths and weaknesses. Further, the value of these strengths and weaknesses will vary according to the situation. This may be illustrated by reference to the studies of Lupton (1963). Lupton studied productivity standards in shop-floor workgroups in two British factories. His research method was participant observation; in other words he worked alongside the employees in each factory for a period of months.

Lupton found that in one factory ('Jays'), which was engaged in light engineering in Manchester, there was a restrictive work standard, which everyone referred to as the 'fiddle'. In the other factory ('Wye'), which was engaged in the manufacture of waterproof garments in South Wales, there was an expectation that each employee would seek to maximize his or her individual earnings. Thus one of his cases replicated the Bank Wiring study's findings while the other did not. Lupton analyses a broad range of possible reasons why different standards should prevail in the two shops. At Jays' there was a stable market, interdependent work, a history of union organization, predominantly male workers and relatively low labour costs. At Wye, on the other hand, there was a small unstable market, independent tasks, a weak union, predominantly female workers and high labour costs. Most likely all of these factors contributed to the different work standards. To work very hard at Jays' would be independent and to respond to disapproval of this by working still harder would be anticonformity. To do so would maximize one's short-term earnings at the expense of weakening the bargaining position of one's workmates. Similar behaviour at Wye would be conformity however, and would be accepted, possibly because short-term gain is valued more highly than long-term stability in that setting. To take this analysis further, one would need more data from the two factories, as to who compared their wages with whose and what values were salient in each setting.

Our analysis of the consequences of social comparison has so far described what some of the consequences may be. Nothing has been reported which attempts to predict which of the various consequences will occur when. Dissonance theory is a step in this direction, but it is not sufficiently specific at present to make unequivocal predictions. A model somewhat related to dissonance theory has been proposed by Adams (1965), which is oriented towards trying to specify the conditions under which people experience equity. One of the striking findings of the Hawthorne studies was the evidence of widely shared norms as to what constituted a 'fair day's work for a fair day's pay'. Adams's work may be seen as an attempt to pin down these norms and show how they operate.

Adams's theory is directly concerned with the outcome of social comparisons. According to him one compares the ratio of one's 'inputs' to 'outcomes' with the ratio achieved by comparison others. If the comparison indicates inequity, one attempts to reduce that inequity. Adams refers to anyone who experiences equity or inequity as 'Person' and to the individual with whom Person compares himself as 'Other'.

Person's inputs are any attributes which Person himself sees as being relevant to his performance. They often include age, seniority, skill, training and effort. Adams stresses that some of these variables may not be perceived as inputs by Other or by employers; none the less we are concerned about the situation from Person's point of view, not theirs. Person's outcomes are the benefits he derives from his performance. They may include pay, intrinsic satisfaction in doing a task, status recognition, good relationships and so on. As with inputs, we are concerned with how Person sees his outcomes not with how others see them. The Adams model asserts that if the ratio of Person's inputs to outcomes differs from Person's perception of Other's input/outcome ratio, then Person will experience inequity. Inequity, like dissonance, is uncomfortable, and Person will seek to reduce it. Note that the Adams model makes no distinction between inequity where Person is overcompensated and inequity where he is undercompensated. In other words, the model states that people will be as uneasy about being overpaid as they would be about being underpaid, for example. One of the reasons why Adams's model has attracted attention is that at some points, such as on overpayment, its predictions contradict common sense. If their predictions can be upheld, theories which do more than reinforce received common sense are obviously to be preferred.

A number of interesting experiments have been reported which test aspects of equity theory (Goodman and Friedman, 1971; Pritchard, 1969). Most of the experiments are based on the manipulation of the input side of the equation. Students are hired to work on a task, such as proof-reading. They are then led to believe that they are either well-qualified or poorly qualified to do the task and paid at various different rates for the same work. This procedure rather circumvents the process of social comparison. The subject is not provided with a comparison other, but is instead told by the experimenter that he is being paid the rate for the job, or the rate for a more highly skilled person, etc. Adams and Jacobsen (1964) found that when subjects were paid on piece-rate, their overpaid subjects worked more slowly but more thoroughly. Adams and Rosenbaum (1962) report that on an hourly pay rate, the overpaid subjects worked the fastest. Both sets of findings are consistent with the theory.

Friedman and Goodman (1967) suggest that when a subject is told by the experimenter that he is overpaid, this may do more than simply affect his perceived inputs. He may receive the comments as an affront to his self-esteem and seek to disprove the experimenter's negative image of him, if his previous experience in employment leads him to see himself as well-qualified. If he does not have much previous experience, he may simply accept the experimenter's viewpoint. Friedman and Goodman found that the overpayment effect was in fact only obtained for those subjects who initially saw themselves as well-qualified. Equity theory cannot explain this finding.

Pritchard (1969) concludes that experiments with equity theory have consistently supported the predictions concerning the effect of underpayment. But the effects obtained with overpayment can more plausibly be put down to the experimental methods used. Where the subject has been 'insulted', i.e. told he is underqualified, the overpayment effects do occur, but where alternative methods are used (Andrews, 1967) the effect disappears. Pritchard proposes some reformulations of equity theory to take account of this. The most important point is that Adams's theory is concerned primarily with equity between Person and Other. Yet in the instance of wage equity there is always an important third party to the transaction, namely the employer. It is very probable that if one is overpaid one might argue that this was the employer's fault. Only if one perceived a direct one-to-one connection between Person being overpaid and Other consequently being paid less would equity norms prevail. Although Adams does acknowledge the importance of third parties, his theory does not go into the manner in which they affect the situation. Equity theory therefore needs reformulation to take account of the 'third-party' component of any exchange relationship.

This line of argument is reminiscent of Patchen's findings, discussed earlier. It will be recalled that those who choose dissonant comparison others were those who tended to believe that advancement in the organization was not dependent on personal initiative but on decisions made by the hierarchy. Likewise in exchange if Person sees no relation between his outcomes and Other's outcomes, equity theory will have little to say; but if Person sees Other's outcomes as contingent on his own outcomes, then the theory will have a great deal to say.

The consequences of social comparison are thus still difficult to predict. The laboratory experiments have concerned themselves with only a few of the possible ways in which one might seek to reduce inequity. Changes in rate or quality of work have been selected as measures because they are easier to measure. But Adams's theory can only be wholly tested if one takes into account also the other possible modes of inequity reduction which he specifies. These include changing the perceived value of particular inputs or outcomes, changing one's comparison other and leaving the situation altogether. Each of these would be difficult to study experimentally, but could be important in more long-term organizations.

Having arrived almost at the end of the present chapter, it may be helpful to reflect on the relationship between the process of social comparison, with which we have so far been concerned, and other forms of social influence, to which we shall turn next. If we persevere with Adams's terms, social comparison is a process in which Person voluntarily uses Other as a guideline or marker post against which to evaluate himself. He may do this because he is uncertain of himself, or because he is seeking to maintain the equity of his outcomes. Both uncertainty and concern about one's outcomes are widespread, so the effects of social comparison are quite marked in groups and in organizations. But social comparison is a process centred on Person. He chooses Other and he decides what to do in the light of the results of his comparison. In the next chapter we look at the inverse situation where Other tries to influence how Person behaves. From our view of Person trying to find some guidelines for his behaviour, we turn to Other's difficulties in trying to control Person.

Summary

The process of social comparison can most easily be demonstrated in a situation where a person is uncertain of himself. Ambiguity and hence uncertainty is widespread, both in the psychology laboratory but also in long-term groups and organizations. Hence the process of social comparison is frequently encountered.

In the face of uncertainty, Person seeks out one or more Others with whom he can compare himself on relevant attributes. Usually but not always he will choose someone as similar to himself as possible. Patchen's work in oil-refineries indicates that one may also engage in processes of social comparison, when one is not uncertain about oneself, but rather when important sources of reward are at stake.

The consequences of social comparison are likely to be a reduction in ambiguity, coupled with either confirmations or disconfirmations of one's beliefs or behaviours. These confirmations and disconfirmations will serve to develop and maintain in groups and in organizations agreed norms concerning which behaviours are highly valued and which are rejected. The norms which develop concerning productivity for example may be restrictive or may not be, depending on the specific circumstances.

Adams's equity theory is an attempt to predict the consequences of social comparisons. So far it has shown itself better able to explain the consequences of underpayment than of overpayment.

III The Exercise of Control

This chapter, like the last one, will begin with an account of a series of experiments focused on electric shock. One should not infer from this that most small group studies are to do with shocks, nor even that the more important studies are. It just so happens that these two series of experiments serve to highlight in a vivid manner the processes to be explored in these chapters. The basic procedure in the present series (Milgram, 1963; 1964a, b; 1965a, b) was for the experimenter to instruct the subject to administer a series of electric shocks to another subject. The experiment was presented as a study of learning and the subject was instructed to give a shock every time the learner made a mistake. The shocks were arranged in a rising series, such that each was more intense than the previous one. After reading the last chapter the reader will no longer be surprised to learn that no actual shocks were administered. None the less Milgram's accounts of his work make it clear that his experiments were so convincingly staged that the experimental subjects certainly believed that they were administering real shocks.

Milgram's purpose was to make a study of obedience. By varying the parameters of the experiment, he sought to determine the conditions under which someone would blindly carry out the orders of another, even when the task was an objectionable one and the orders were unsupported by any kind of reasoning. These experiments are among the most controversial to have been conducted by social psychologists to date. Critics (e.g. Baumrind, 1964; Kelman, 1968) have questioned whether researchers have the right to impose on their subjects the kind of stress which Milgram's subjects undoubtedly faced in deciding whether or not to disobey their orders. Furthermore, studies of such destructive forms of obedience are open to misuse by totalitarian authority. Milgram's reply (1964a) is that when his subjects discovered what had happened they were predominantly glad to have learned something about themselves. He sees his research as reducing rather than enhancing the threat of totalitarian authority systems. If we know the conditions under which blind obedience to authority arises, we are better placed to limit its incidence. Debate about the permissible limits of experimentation is likely to continue.

The subjects were faced with a large electric-shock generator with a dial calibrated from 15 to 450 volts. At several points on the dial were inserted designations ranging from 'slight shock' to 'Danger: severe shock'. The learner is strapped into a chair in preparation for receiving his shocks. A series of tape-recordings simulating reactions from the learner are played when particular shock levels are reached. For example, at 75 volts he grunts and moans; at 150 volts he demands to be let out; at 180 volts he states that he can no longer stand the pain; at higher levels he pounds the wall or screams with pain, and later becomes silent. Milgram's central finding was quite unexpected: he had anticipated that most subjects would quickly refuse to proceed farther than the moderate shock levels. In fact twenty-six of the forty subjects continued giving shocks right up to the maximum point on the scale. How was this level of obedience obtained? At all points where the subject wavered, the experimenter said simply, 'You have no other choice, you must go on.' Milgram hypothesized that the effect might have something to do with the prestige of Yale University, where the experiments were conducted. When he repeated the experiment in a seedy, anonymous building in a nearby town, the percentage of totally obedient subjects fell from sixty-five to forty-eight per cent. A second possible variant explored was the physical presence of the experimenter. Where he was only in telephone communication with the subject, twenty-three per cent of subjects were totally obedient, compared with sixty-five per cent when he was present in person. In addition subjects frequently lied over the telephone, stating that they had administered high shocks when they had not in fact done so. The third set of variations concerned how much contact the subject had with his victim. Where the victim was neither visible nor audible, sixty-five per cent were obedient; where he could be heard but not seen, sixty-two per cent were obedient; where the victim sat beside the subject, forty per cent were obedient; finally, where the subject had to place the victim's hand on the shock-plate, thirty per cent were still totally obedient.

Thus the experimenter's success in obtaining obedience fluctuated considerably depending on the circumstances. One variable Milgram did not change was money: all subjects were paid $4.50 before the experiment began. Subjects in all the experiments were men aged twenty to fifty years drawn from the New Haven area and with a social class distribution approximating the general population. We may conclude that the effectiveness of Milgram's experimenters in obtaining obedience rested on money, the prestige of Yale, the personal presence of the experimenter and the remoteness of the victim.

In reading this account of Milgram's work, the reader may have had occasion to think back to the previous chapter. Is not the Milgram paradigm another novel situation, like Schachter's study, where the subject would feel very unsure of himself and look for guidance through social comparison? One of the striking things about the experimental setting is that the subject is in a situation where demands are made on him while he has no comparison other available. As such it is rather unlike situations that arise within organizations. In further variations of his experiment, Milgram (1964b) investigated the effect of introducing such comparison others. In one study three subjects were asked to collaborate in deciding the level of shocks to be administered. Two of the group were accomplices of the experimenter and they suggested steadily higher shock levels. The subjects went along with these suggestions to a considerable degree, even though subjects deciding by themselves showed no such trend to increase shock levels. This experiment therefore shows how social comparison can induce conformity towards increased shock. But there is no authority figure in the design, so that we cannot compare the effects of social comparison with those of control.

In another version groups of three received instructions from the experimenter to administer the usual series of steadily increasing shocks. The two accomplices never queried their instructions. Under these conditions total obedience by the subject rose slightly to seventy-two per cent. This is not markedly different from the sixty-five per cent figure where the subject is on his own. In other words where social comparison points the same way as the authority figure, not much effect is found.

The final version of this study (Milgram, 1965a) was one in which the two accomplices refused to continue carrying out the orders of the experimenter. Their refusals occurred at separate points on the scale of mounting shock intensity. Under these conditions a mere ten per cent of the subjects showed total obedience. Thus social comparison may play an exceedingly important part in limiting the potency of controlling demands from authority figures. The example given by the refusal of the two accomplices to accept orders was more powerful in reducing obedience than any of the other variations.

This final version of the Milgram experiment offers a much

closer parallel with non-experimental settings than the earlier ones. The subject is exposed to contradictory indications from different sources. A powerful authority demands that he behave in one way, while concurrently his comparison others do not accept these demands. This contradiction is reminiscent of the Bank Wiring study and of many other workgroups in large organizations. Many analysts of organizational behaviour have found it useful to distinguish what they term 'formal' organization from 'informal' organization. Formal organization constitutes the obligations and demands which organization members are entitled to make on one another. Informal organization is not prescribed but comprises other forms of influence which arise within the organization and hence limit and augment the effects of formal organization. This distinction relates to the present analysis since social comparison processes will be a major determinant of informal organization, while the exercise of control constitutes the essence of formal organization. Social comparison processes are those where the organization member orients his behaviour in relation to others, while control processes are those where others deliberately attempt to influence his behaviour.

One should not assume that social comparison processes always have the capacity to nullify the effects of control processes, as they did in the final version of the Milgram experiment. A precondition for this may be that the leader's demands are unreasonable. An experiment by Helmreich and Collins (1967) tested the relative attractiveness of leadership and social comparison in the Schachter-type shock experiment. In the social comparison conditions, subjects were told that they would work on tasks individually, but in the presence of two others while awaiting the shock experiment. In the leader condition they were told that there would be in addition a leader who would assign tasks and direct performance. The original Schachter study did not of course offer subjects the chance of waiting with leaders. In the Helmreich and Collins study it was found that subjects actually preferred to wait with leaders. It thus modifies the earlier conclusions and makes it a little easier to see how the two processes of social comparison and control will be interrelated where both are operative.

The Milgram studies have been described at length because they pose in a rather pointed manner the problem of why we accord to certain others the right to tell us how to behave. We shall explore two issues: firstly, under what circumstances is someone accorded this right? and secondly, what do we know about the conditions under which this right is most effectively exercised?

Acquiring the right to control

The traditional or common-sense view of the process of control has been that it passes to those who have a particular combination of personality traits. Some of us are 'born leaders' while others are not. This view has been strongly discredited by research. A detailed summary by Mann (1959) reviews the findings of several hundred earlier studies. The most studied relationship is that between intelligence and leadership. Of 196 occasions when this relation has been tested it has been positive in 173 separate tests. Thus there *is* a tendency for leadership and intelligence to go together. But, as Mann reports, the median value of correlations between intelligence and leadership in these studies is only +0·25. This is equivalent to saying that only about six per cent of the variance in leader behaviour is accounted for by variations in intelligence. In a similar manner measures of dominance relate to attainment of leadership (median correlation +0·20); as do measures of adjustment (+0·15) and extroversion (+0·15). We must conclude that while each of these measures can account for a few per cent of the variance in leadership, the overall picture is not one of a certain type of 'ideal' leader personality.

The view of the process of control which has replaced the discredited theory of ideal types is usually known as the 'situational' theory. According to this the people whom we are prepared to accept as leaders will differ from one situation to another. We follow the lead of someone highly intelligent when faced with a difficult problem, of someone familiar with the locality when visiting a strange place, of someone friendly in a social setting or of a policeman in a traffic accident. Such a model of leadership is inherently plausible but somewhat too vague to be of great use. It is always possible to look at situations, see whose leadership is most accepted and then analyse *post hoc* why their contribution should have been most valued in that particular setting. What is needed is approaches which will tell us in advance what type of leadership will be accepted in which setting.

Hollander and Julian (1971) have reported a series of studies which attempt to make progress in this direction. In one experiment subjects were presented with hypothetical descriptions of leaders and asked to imagine themselves in a group led by such a person. Their ratings of these hypothetical leaders turned out to be higher when the leader was described as a 'good performer in the group activity'. They were also somewhat higher if the leader was 'interested in group activities' and if he was 'interested in group members'. On the other hand it made no difference whether the leader was described as elected or appointed. In experiments where experimentally composed groups worked on a judgement task it was again found that competence was the strongest determinant of how much influence the leader had. Our confidence in this finding is strengthened since it is obtained through the use of two quite different research methods.

Hollander's conceptualization of the leadership process derives from a more broadly formulated position, usually known as exchange theory (Homans, 1961; Thibaut and Kelley, 1959). Exchange theorists postulate that we seek to maximize the outcomes we derive from our relations to others and they attempt to analyse this in a quasi-economic manner. Thus a leader who is competent is more likely to generate rewards for his followers and therefore is more likely to be accepted as a source of control. Hollander attends not only to the degree of task competence the potential leader displays but also the degree to which he conforms to the views of his followers. He argues that in order to achieve leadership status in the first instance the aspirant leader may well have to conform to the expectations of the group or organization; but in order to retain leadership status, it may be equally necessary to resist conformity pressures. This is because leaders who are accepted are those who achieve the results: if achieving results requires that the leader resists group conformity pressures, the group will accept this. Pursuing his exchange theory viewpoint, Hollander argues that the leader will build up 'idiosyncrasy credit'. In other words, because of past success the group will tolerate present non-conformity; but if present non-conformity does not generate further group success, then the leader's idiosyncrasy credit will be reduced and in future he will have to work within more constraining limits. Thus a heroic leader might enjoy considerable liberty, while a leader whose status was marginal might be virtually the prisoner of his group's demands. In an ingenious laboratory experiment, Hollander (1960) showed that followers tolerated more non-conformity from their leader on an experimental laboratory task if the leader had earlier both conformed and shown himself competent. Hollander and Julian (1971) found that elected leaders were more likely not to conform subsequently than were appointed leaders.

Hollander's emphasis on competence and conformity as crucial determinants of leadership is reminiscent of earlier work by Bales and his associates at Harvard (Bales, 1958; Slater, 1955). These workers argued that any group is faced with the problem of keeping in balance the demands which the task imposes on the group and the need for socio-emotional cohesion in the group. They were able to show that under certain circumstances experimental groups tended to develop a divided leadership structure whereby one member became a 'task specialist', while a second was a 'socio-emotional' specialist. While Bales's work was centred on the conditions under which such a split arises, Hollander attends instead to the conditions under which a single leader succeeds in holding these contradictory pressures in balance. Neither project can say anything to us about which style of leadership is more effective, and we shall be turning to this presently. What they do instead is to delineate some of the factors determining who fills available leadership roles. Verba (1961) has suggested that the split which Bales found between task and socio-emotional specialists will be found only in *ad hoc* short-term experiments. Some confirmation of this was obtained by Smith (1963), who showed that among management training groups there was less of a split the more cohesive was the group.

The experimenter in the Milgram studies showed no obvious signs of competence or conformity. Indeed, he avoided the use of reasoned arguments or any revelation of his own opinions. He was obeyed simply because the subjects conceded that he had the *right* to give orders. While competence and conformity will always enter into the determination of leadership status, many leaders, particularly those in organizations, are obeyed primarily because they have the right to give orders. The Hollander and Julian (1971) studies referred to already included a distinction between leaders who were elected and those who were appointed and found no difference in their acceptance by followers. This may well be because both modes of appointment were legitimate ones in the experimental setting. In order to show the power of legitimation as a determinant of leadership, it is necessary to include within the study some leaders who are illegitimately appointed. Such a study was conducted by Raven and French (1958). Subjects worked on a task in groups and each group contained an accomplice of the experimenter. In one condition of the experiment this stooge was appointed leader by a rigged election, while in another condition she simply took over the group without formal election. The leader's influence was found to be much greater where she was appointed.

In summary, we are more likely to grant others the right to control our behaviour where they are competent at relevant tasks, where their behaviour conforms to our preferences and where they have been appointed to the task of control in a manner we accept as legitimate. None of these bases are sovereign and all are weakened if the others are not in support. Where all these bases for influence concur, the leader will indeed be powerful. But since the different bases are more often incompatible than in support of one another, leaders are more often aware of their impotence than of their power. Let us examine some reasons why this should be so.

The leader as middleman

Many leaders depend more on one of these sources of influence than the others. For example a leader might lean heavily on his legitimacy as a source of influence, stressing his *right* to give orders to others. In this instance he runs the risk of exceeding the idiosyncrasy credit the subordinate group is prepared to accord him. An 'informal organization' with its own style of leadership will arise to oppose him and to preserve the values of the subordinate group. This process was clearly illustrated in the group condition of the Milgram experiment. It may also have occurred in Bales's group discussions. If the process of control is pitted against the process of social comparison, the leader cannot rely on control being the stronger of the two.

An alternative possibility would be for the leader to seek to stress his essential similarity to his subordinates. If he conforms to their wishes to a sufficient degree, he may himself become a basis for social comparison. The Hollander model of idiosyncrasy credit indicates how this might occur. In such a manner the leader would remain leader and yet not be in conflict with the social comparison processes within his subordinate group. If this were always a practical possibility then the distinction argued in this book between processes of control and processes of social comparison would be much weakened. It would become much simpler to argue instead that there is but one effective influence process. However, the possibility of a leader making himself the basis of social comparison is severely constrained. The more that his behaviour is orientated towards his subordinate group, the more it is likely to be at odds with the directions proposed by more senior management groups who legitimate his occupancy of a leadership role in the first place. Senior management will put pressure on him to behave more in accord with their priorities and less in accord with those of his subordinates.

Leadership thus constitutes a balancing process. It is not simply a matter of passing on the control demands of one's superiors nor of accommodating to the social comparison processes of one's subordinates. It is the occupancy of a role uniquely situated between two or more groups within an organization. The major attempt to conceptualize this 'linking-pin' role is that of Likert (1961) which has already been referred to. Likert's book *New Patterns of Management* remains the most coherent exposition of the 'human relations' school of thought whose work at the University of Michigan has formed much of the basis for the linking-pin theory. Likert surveys data from studies conducted within a variety of organizations. In each case the goal was the same: to identify differences between supervisors whose subordinates were relatively highly productive and those whose subordinates were less so. Studies were conducted in insurance, railway maintenance gangs, a tractor factory, government research laboratories, voluntary organizations and elsewhere. The basic findings can be summarized under three headings. The most competent supervisors were:

(1) more active in tasks which differentiated them from their subordinates. They spent more time planning ahead and training others, but less time working alongside their subordinates.
(2) less frequent in checking up on their subordinates' performance.
(3) more likely to be perceived by their subordinates as 'employee-oriented' than as 'production-oriented'. In other words, in disputes with higher management they were seen as more likely to stand by their employees than to side with higher management.

These findings indicate Likert's view that competent supervision leans more on paying attention to the subordinate group than on emphasizing one's organizational right to give orders. Indeed, the second and third findings specifically indicate ways in which the supervisor's conformity to his subordinates' preferences is more important than his organizational legitimacy.

The Likert findings contradict some versions of generally accepted common sense. The best managers, the second and third findings seem to say, are those who spend less time managing. The bulk of Likert's data is such that the findings command attention. Since the publication of the data a powerful critique of them has been developed by various authors (Strauss, 1963; Lowin, 1968) which we shall now examine. The effect of the critique is not to destroy the value of the Michigan work, but to point to some limitations of the generality of its applicability.

The first criticism of the Michigan work is that it was done at Michigan. Such a criticism may seem unduly small-minded. The basis for it is that the University of Michigan has considerable renown as a centre of research into human-relations aspects of organizations. There is most unlikely to be any wish among research workers at Michigan to study a biased sample of organizations, but the possibility remains that the reputation of Michigan will selectively bias the sample of organizations making contact with them. In view of this possibility, one should be on the look-out as to whether researchers at other institutions obtain comparable findings. In this instance Fiedler, at the University of Illinois, was obtaining contradictory findings throughout the 1950s. We shall examine his work presently.

A second problem with the Likert model is that it assumes a linear relationship between the various dimensions of supervisor behaviour and subordinate performance. This is nowhere spelled out precisely, but the data are laid out in such a manner as to suggest for example that the more employee-oriented the supervisor is the higher will be subordinate performance. There is clearly a point beyond which this kind of relationship becomes most improbable. There is much more likely to be some kind of threshold beyond which further increments in supervisor employee-orientedness do not affect the subordinate, or even reduce his performance by creating conflicts with senior management's control demands. Fleishman and Harris (1962) report such curvilinear relationships between the supervisor's consideration and the subordinate's response and between the degree to which the supervisor initiates and the subordinate's response. Some of their graphs are reproduced as Figure 2. The fact that such curvilinear relationships have been rarely found is almost certainly because they had been only rarely sought.

The Michigan studies are based on surveys rather than experiments. In other words, the researchers made no attempt to change the supervisor's behaviour experimentally: they merely recorded the correlations between supervisor behaviour and subordinate performance. Herein lies the weakness of all survey research: one has no way of knowing what causes what. Likert asserts that it is supervisor behaviour which causes subordinate performance. But is it not equally plausible that subordinate performance influences supervisor behaviour? As with many aspects of interpersonal behaviour one might expect some kind of cyclical feedback whereby each persons's behaviour affected the other's. Lowin and Craig (1968) used a role-playing stooge to test the hypothesis that the subordinate can influence his supervisor's behaviour. They found that the stooges who worked hard caused their supervisors to be more considerate, less initiating and more close than did the indolent stooges. Thus all that Likert's data establishes is that there *may* be a causal link between the supervisor's behaviour and subordinate performance.

In order to test the direction of causation more rigorously we must turn to those few experiments which the Michigan group have conducted which are relevant to this point. In each of these

FIGURE 2 *Relationships between labour turnover in the supervisor's section and the supervisor's consideration and initiation of structure**

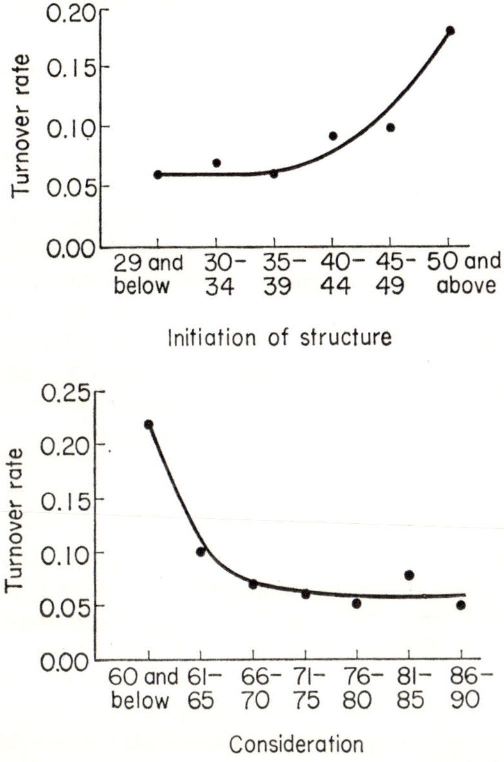

* Taken from Fleishman and Harris (see reference p. 123. Used with permission of *Personnel Psychology*). The measures of supervision behaviour are based on questionnaires completed by the supervisor.

experiments the supervisor's behaviour is deliberately changed and the consequences of this are assessed by measurement of subordinates' behaviour. The findings are mixed. A classic study by Coch and French (1948) showed enhanced production after the introduction of changes by way of group discussion. An attempt by French, Israel and As (1960) to replicate this finding was unsuccessful. Likert (1961) reports an experiment in which supervisors were reassigned to different sections and each section's productivity changed in response to the new supervisor towards the levels found in the supervisor's former section. An ambitious experiment by Morse and Reimer (1956), which involved training half the supervisors in an insurance firm to centralize decision-making and the other half to decentralize, resulted in large productivity increases in both conditions. Differences were found in morale under the two systems, but one should probably not conclude too much from this study as, since there was only a finite amount of work, increased productivity implied increased redundancy.

It is exceedingly difficult to control extraneous variations in field experiments such as these. The consequence of this is that it is usually possible to argue (Lowin, 1968) that even the positive findings are interpretable in other terms. The conclusion most favouring Likert's position from these experiments could be phrased no more strongly than that under *some* circumstances an increase in participative or employee-centred supervision causes increased subordinate performance. An alternative way of phrasing it would be to say that the experimental evidence is consistent with the view that different situations call for a different balance between the supervisor controlling through his legitimate authority and the supervisor influencing through making himself a basis for social comparison by his subordinates.

The contingency model of leadership effectiveness

Although Likert's model incorporates a sophisticated view of linkages between groups in organizations, in one way it resembles the discredited 'trait' theory of leadership. It asserts that there is one best way to lead in all situations. It should come as no surprise therefore that Likert's theory is only supported in some settings. Vroom (1960) found that among workers in a packaging plant authoritarians preferred authoritarian supervisors, while non-authoritarians preferred participative supervisors. Goldthorpe *et al.* (1968) found that among assembly-line workers in a British car factory, the preferred type of supervisor was someone who left one alone. Such diversity is not assimilable into any prescriptive theory which asserts that there is one right way to lead effectively.

Earlier in this chapter we examined how different people become selected as leaders in different settings. Fiedler's theory (1967) attempts to make situational leadership theory more cogent by specifying the conditions under which these various types of leaders will be more or less effective. This is an ambitious enterprise which necessarily involves Fiedler in making quite a few simplifications. For example, he assumes that the effectiveness of leaders is validly measured by the productivity of their subordinates, ignoring morale and other indicators. He assumes furthermore that the leader's qualities need to be classified on only a single dimension. Finally he assumes that situations in which leaders operate can be classified in terms of their favourability to the leader.

Fiedler's theory arose out of his work in the 1950s. Like the Michigan researchers, he was engaged in survey studies, using a variety of settings, which were in his case open-hearth steel mills, basket-ball league teams, military units, agricultural co-operatives and so forth. In most of these settings he found that a more aloof, controlling leader was more effective than a warmer relationship-orientated leader. Thus his findings appeared to contradict those of the Michigan workers. However, both the settings he studied and the measures he used were different.

The model which Fiedler developed is portrayed in Figure 3.

FIGURE 3 *Fiedler's model of leadership effectiveness*

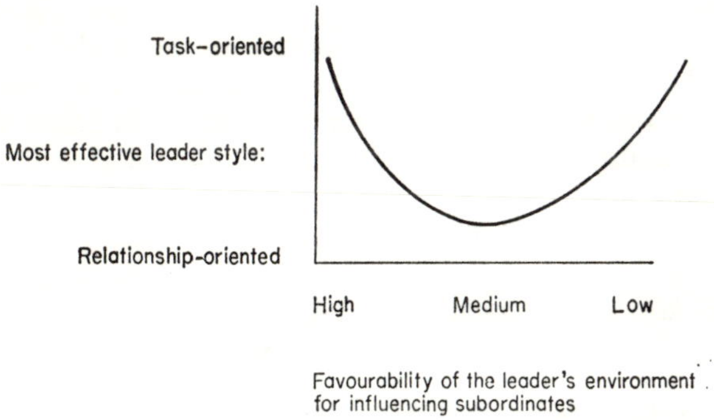

Let us consider three points on his graph. Where the situation is highly favourable to the leader, it is easy for him to influence his followers. His right to control their behaviour is firmly established. Hence directive, task-oriented leadership will work best in this type of situation; it is less elaborate and time-consuming than more participative methods. Where the situation is moderately favourable to the leader, he is faced with some reluctance in his followers. They will only permit him to control them if he goes some way towards meeting their needs in return. In this situation Fiedler postulates that the relationship-orientated, more personal style of leadership will be superior. The third point on Fiedler's graph to be considered is that where the situation is unfavourable to the leader. Here he has very few bases on which to rest his influence and certainly no possibility of meeting their needs. Fiedler argues that all he can do is depend on whatever coercive power he does have. Consequently, directive, task-oriented leader-

FIGURE 4 *Likert's model of leadership effectiveness interpreted in terms of Fiedler's concepts*

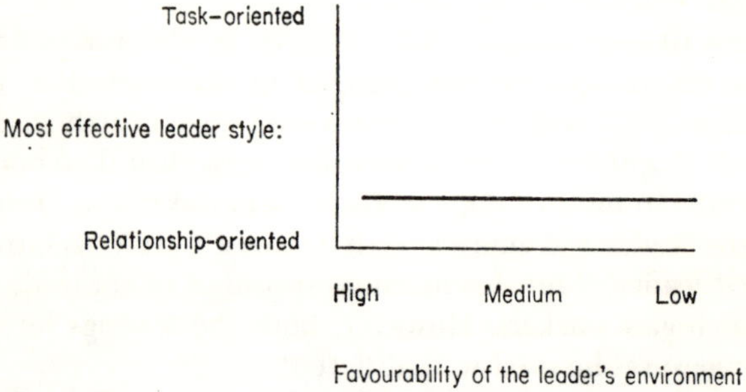

ship is once again the more effective. The overall model therefore predicts a 'U'-shaped curvilinear relation between leadership style and leadership effectiveness.

Fiedler's curvilinear model contrasts with the models of Likert and Hollander which we have already examined. For comparison the Likert and Hollander models are presented in graph form in Figures 4 and 5. For Likert, relationship-orientated leadership is

FIGURE 5 *Hollander's model of leadership effectiveness*

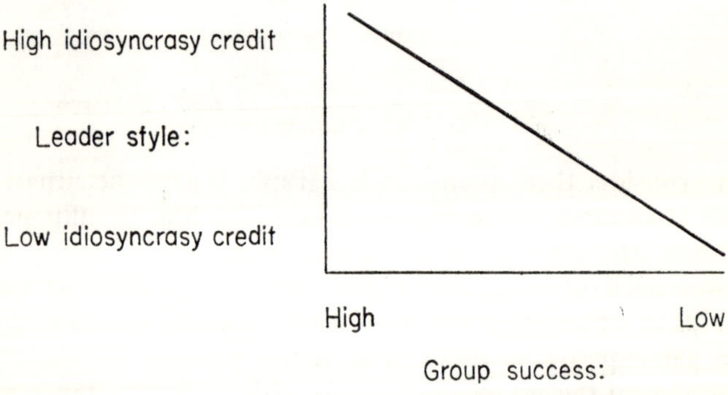

always superior, so his graph comes out as a straight line. Likert's model thus appears to contradict the Fiedler model, but his data need not necessarily do so. If one could show that Likert's data were all derived from situations of medium favourability to leaders, then Fiedler's model and Likert's model would make the same prediction that relationship-orientated leadership was superior. We have not yet discussed how Fiedler ascertains the favourability of a situation for a leader, but needless to say Fiedler's measures are not available for Likert's studies, so we are unable to test whether these were in medium-favourable situations.

Hollander's model is laid out graphically in Figure 5. The leader's idiosyncrasy credit declines linearly as the group's success declines. In order to relate this to the Fiedler model we have to assume that settings favourable to their leaders will produce more group success and that one of the ways in which a leader in such groups might use his idiosyncrasy credit is in imposing 'unreasonable' task demands on his followers. In other words, a leader high on idiosyncrasy credit could afford to be controlling and directive, whereas a leader low on idiosyncrasy credit would have to meet the needs of his followers by being more relationship-orientated. If this parallel between the two models is correct, then Hollander's model resembles the left-hand side of Fiedler's. According to Hollander, below a certain level of success the leader simply ceases to be leader. Fiedler's research has been more concerned with formal work organizations; under these conditions this is rarely possible in the short run. However discredited, the leader always retains some vestige of the sanctions he exercises on behalf of the organization.

There are thus both parallels and some apparent differences between the three models of leadership presented. The differences may be more apparent than real since the models were formulated with different kinds of situation in mind. In order to know whether this is so or not, we have to attend to attempts to measure the qualities of different situations. This is precisely the point on which Fiedler's model is most explicit.

Fiedler (1967) outlines three dimensions along which situations can be said to vary in favourability for the leader's influence attempts. The most important of these is postulated to be the warmth of leader–follower relationships. Fiedler maintains that where the leader's relation to his followers is warm and friendly the situation is more favourable for influence by the leader than if his relations are cool and distant. The second most important dimension is that of task structure. Where the task is a structured one, it should be much easier for the leader to see whether it is being done correctly or not. Where the task is more diffuse, his situation is less favourable. The third dimension identified by Fiedler is the amount of power inherent in the leader's position. Some leaders are endowed with a great many sanctions and rewards which they may administer to their followers, while others are not. Again, the leader who has more position power is said to be in a more favourable position.

The three dimensions of leadership situations delineated by Fiedler certainly sound likely to be important in determining the leader's ability to influence his followers. It is important to note, however, that Fiedler's selection of these dimensions is an essentially arbitrary one. No theoretical rationale for the choice is provided in the 1967 book. Indeed, in later writings Fiedler has tended to adduce further dimensions as being important also. Later in his book, in discussing an important test of his model made with Belgian Navy subjects, Fiedler introduces the dimension of group heterogeneity into his analysis. In Fiedler *et al.* (1969) a study was made of the effectiveness of public health teams in Honduras. In this instance, a measure of stress was used also in computing the favourability or unfavourability of the situation. Fiedler's most recent statement (1971a) stands by the utility of the three postulated dimensions and argues that, in the instance of the 1969 study, the effect of stress was to render the task more unstructured.

Controversy surrounds the question of whether the evidence supports Fiedler's contingency model. Graen *et al.* (1970) maintain that although the model looked plausible on the basis of Fiedler's re-analysis of his early research, more recent studies have failed to support the predictions of the model. Fiedler (1971a) denies this. As is often the case in disputes in the behavioural sciences, the issues concern how successful the researchers have been in translating their theoretical models into valid empirical tests. A few examples will illustrate this.

Shaw and Blum (1966) studied the task structure dimension of the model in a laboratory experiment. Groups worked on three different tasks in various sequences. Each group's leader was briefed either to lead in a highly controlling manner or in a more permissive manner. It was found that the groups with controlling leaders did best on the most structured task, while they did worst on the other two less structured tasks. In a general manner, this can be said to support the Fiedler model, although the researchers had been expecting that on the least structured task the situation would be so unfavourable that controlling leaders would do best. Shaw and Blum disposed of the gap between their finding and their expectation, by arguing that they had been wrong to expect that one could create an unfavourable situation in the laboratory simply by manipulating one of the three dimensions in the model.

Graen *et al.* (1971) did attempt to manipulate all three of

Fiedler's dimensions within a single experiment. The findings showed little difference between the effects of leaders' behaviour in the different conditions. Fiedler (1971b) retorts that the Graen experiments did not succeed in creating very much difference between the various situations staged in the laboratory, so that the study is not a valid test of his theory. The data appear to support Fiedler rather than Graen on this point.

Fiedler's own approach to experimental tests of his theory has laid less emphasis on instructing people to play different roles and more on composing groups on the requisite dimensions. For example, in his Belgian Navy study he varied position power by actually having officers as leaders in some groups, but recruits as leaders in the remaining groups. Such approaches are more likely to provide valid tests.

Fiedler's model provides a much-needed focus for thinking about the situational determinants of leadership effectiveness. The tests made of it to date do not yet compel us to reject it. On the other hand, its formulation is so arbitrary that some aspects of it at least are very likely to be shown wrong in due course. It is a valuable model because it has provided the stimulus to search for improvements, which the previous vaguer theories did not.

In one aspect, Fiedler's model is certainly lacking. His measure of leadership style is based on a questionnaire in which the leader is asked to make ratings of someone 'with whom you can work best' and someone else 'with whom you can work least well'. If the respondent describes both people in relatively similar terms, he is categorized as relationship-orientated; on the other hand, if he draws a large distinction between them he is categorized as more controlling and directive. This is because someone who sees a large difference between the two people he is describing must necessarily see the one he cannot work with in more negative terms than someone who sees few differences. Hence he is more likely to be punitive or intolerant of the poor worker. The weakness of this measure is that it implies that a given leader has a fixed, invariant style of leadership which he uses in all situations. There is, however, a great deal of evidence that leaders tend to adapt their behaviour to situations as they arise. Furthermore, Fiedler's measures of leader style have been found not to correlate strongly with other questionnaire measures of leader style, even where there are theoretical grounds to expect such correlations. Of course this is just as likely to be due to weaknesses in the other questionnaires as in Fiedler's measure.

Fiedler (1972) has considered the manner in which those scoring high and low on his measures might vary their behaviour in different types of circumstance. He suggests that those who on his measure appear controlling and directive may in fact become relationship-orientated in favourable settings. Conversely those who appear relationship-orientated may become controlling and directive in highly favourable settings. These apparently surprising suggestions arise from a consideration by Fiedler of the nature of his questionnaire. The major part of his measure derived from asking the subject to describe someone he can 'work least well with', i.e. an unfavourable situation. This could explain why the measure does not relate well to other types of questionnaire. In unfavourable circumstances Fiedler expects the leader's behaviour to be an expression of his most important needs, whereas in more favoured circumstances leaders will be able to attend also to their secondary needs. In this way the situation will interact with the needs of different types of leaders. Fiedler quotes some evidence in support of these views.

Fiedler's thinking on this point has something in common with the ideas looked at earlier in this chapter. It was argued that leaders are faced with the need to keep in balance the exercise of control on behalf of their superiors and keeping in touch with the social comparison processes of their subordinates. To the extent that a leader emphasizes one of these processes, he creates problems for himself in the other area. Fiedler's new thinking suggests that in favourable situations leaders are more likely to keep the two processes in balance. In less favourable circumstances this is less possible and the leader's behaviour swings in one direction or the other, to the benefit or detriment of his group's effectiveness.

Our discussion is getting rather a long way ahead of what the research data has so far established. It is clear that for these ideas to be tested more satisfactorily better measurement will be required. Such measures will need to examine how leaders actually do behave in given types of situations. They will also need to take much more account of the task competence of the leader. Studies by Hollander and Julian were examined earlier which underlined the importance of this variable, but neither Fiedler's model nor Likert's take very much account of it. Finally, a clearer view will be required of the ways in which the environments of groups and organizations vary. It is to this that we next turn.

Summary

The process of control occurs where Other deliberately seeks to influence Person. In contrived settings where Person is subjected to Other's influence attempts in isolation from any third-party pressures (such as in Milgram's experiments), Other can achieve an astonishing degree of power over Person.

The capacity to exercise control over others is only to a slight extent a product of a particular personality pattern. It is much more strongly determined by a number of situational factors such as whether Other has skills relevant to the particular situation, whether he has or has not been given the legitimate 'right' to influence Person, and whether his own behaviour is in accordance with Person's preferences.

The behaviour of leaders depends upon which of these bases of influence is strongest. While one leader might stress the legitimacy of his right to control others, another might soft-pedal this aspect and stress his identification with the interests of his subordinates. By doing this he seeks to ally the processes of social comparison to those of control.

Likert's link-pin theory argues that such participative leaders are uniformly more effective. The evidence is that this may be so in some settings. Fiedler's theory attempts to specify these conditions. To date the theory has been more provocative than conclusive, but the research has lent some support to the notion that a leader emphasizing the process of control will be most effective in situations which are either very favourable to him or very unfavourable. Intermediate situations are those in which more relationship-orientated leaders will be more effective. Progress in this field has been limited by failure to develop adequately conceptualized research measures.

IV Environmental Constraints on Behaviour

The emphasis of much of this book so far has been on the interpersonal: Person compares himself with Other, or else Other exercises control over Person. To analyse interpersonal processes in such a disembodied manner gives a curious effect. One looks at *how* Person relates to Other, but not at the context within which the relationship occurs.

Any group or organization can be construed as seeking balance with its environment. In a loose sense, environment could be defined as including other groups or organizations with whom relations are maintained, but this topic is reserved for Chapter VI. In this chapter, environment means the physical environment which surrounds any social structure. Large organizations tend to spell out some of their intentions in relating to the environment ('to make a profit', 'to survive or grow', 'to provide a service to the community', etc.), whereas with small groups the intentions may be less explicit. In either case the process may be seen in cyclical terms, as illustrated in Figure 6. The environment limits and constrains the type of group or organization which arises. Groups and organizations in their turn modify their own environments.

This process was well illustrated by Homans (1950) in his analysis of the Bank Wiring room. Within the room two separate cliques arose, which were based on the fact that the workers had relatively invariant seating positions. The clique at the front of the room were wiring up slightly larger telephone banks than the clique at the back. The productivity for the clique at the front was 6,600 connections per day. This happened to be exactly the number of connections required on a single bank of the type they were working on. The workers in the back clique worked on banks that required 6,000 connections. They adhered less well to the 6,600 norm, producing nearer to 6,000 per day. The close proximity of the men enabled quick detection of transgressions from the established norms, and provided plenty of opportunities for exercising sanctions over those who did transgress. Thus the physical disposition of the room facilitated the emergence of restrictive productivity norms. The restrictive norms in their turn acted on the environment, for example by reducing the flow of materials into the room, or at a more general level, by reducing the level of productivity of the organization.

FIGURE 6 *The cyclical interplay of persons, organizations and their environments*

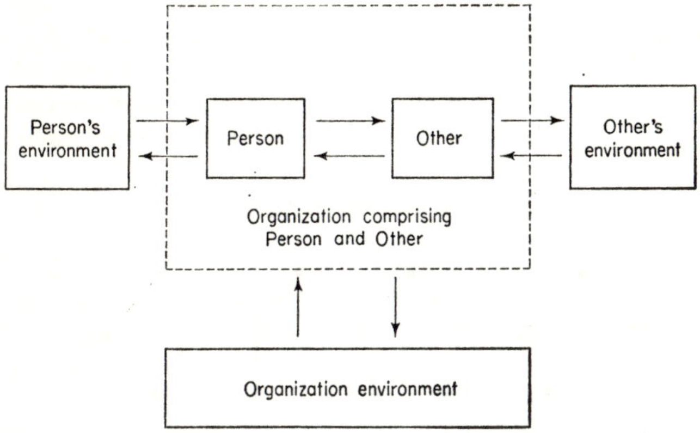

Arrows represent influence processes

In Chapter II of this book Lupton's (1963) study was reported in which it was found that the environment was markedly different where such norms were not operative. Both the Hawthorne analysis by Homans and the Lupton study are descriptive case studies. It will also be recalled that much of Likert's work was criticized earlier, on the grounds that experimental work is necessary if one is to infer what causes what. In examining reported correlations between environment and social structure, we must again pay heed to this necessity.

Communication-net studies

A number of experimental studies have examined the effect of environment on behaviour. Among these are the 'communication-net' studies first devised by Bavelas (1948). In these studies a group of four or five people engage in problem-solving tasks. Various restraints are imposed on their communication patterns and the resultant performance studied. Most typically (Leavitt, 1951) each person receives a list of symbols (e.g. star, circle, wavy line, etc.). Each list is different but all lists contain one symbol in common. The task is to find out as quickly as possible which is the common symbol. The subjects in such experiments are only permitted to communicate with one another by written notes. Furthermore, not everyone can always communicate with everyone. The communication-net studies are obviously rather artificial. Before dismissing them as a source of data, however, one needs to consider what situations they are like and what situations they are not like. Clearly they are not like the small group in which communication is face-to-face and everyone can hear everyone else. They are rather more like situations which arise in large organizations. People in different parts of the organization are in touch with one another only indirectly, or, if directly, then often only by relatively impersonal media such as telephone and

FIGURE 7 *Communication-net patterns used by Leavitt**

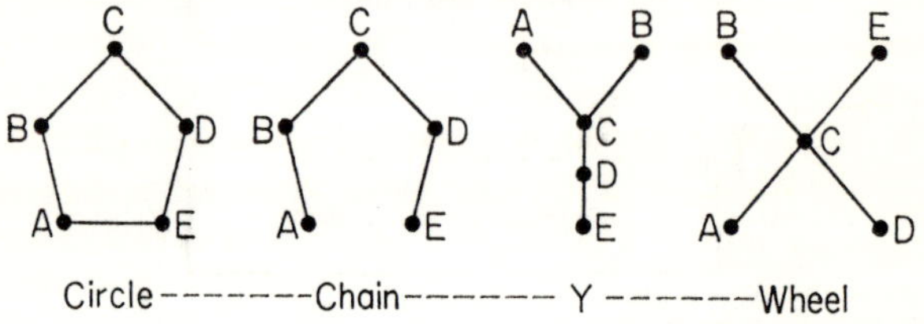

* Taken from H. J. Leavitt, 'Some Effects of Certain Communication Patterns on Group Performance'. *Journal of Abnormal and Social Psychology, 46*, 1951, 38–50. Copyright 1951 by the American Psychological Association, and reproduced by permission.

memorandum, which are not necessarily shared with others. Members of organizations *can* communicate with one another in more personal and direct ways, but quite often they do not have sufficient time to do so.

The communication-networks studied by Leavitt (1951) are shown in Figure 7. Leavitt found that in the more centralized network, which he termed the 'Wheel', the problem was solved more quickly, there were fewer mistakes and fewer messages were required. The man at the centre enjoyed himself much more than the others. Performance in the decentralized network, or 'Circle', was slower, more erratic, but more enjoyable. Members of the wheel groups perceived the central person as leader. This experiment clearly illustrates the manner in which the experimenter's control of the environmental variable affects the emergent social structure. In order to know how much generality these findings have we must examine further studies using a variety of different communication-nets and tasks. Shaw (1964) reviews the outcomes of such studies. He indicates that simple tasks have consistently been done most efficiently in centralized networks such as the wheel. On the other hand, more complex tasks were found to be more effectively performed by less highly centralized networks such as the circle, or a network in which all can communicate with all. The discovery that, by changing the task, one can change the properties of the communication-net, renders these experiments much more interesting. In the last chapter it was indicated (for example in the Shaw and Blum study) that different tasks required different styles of leadership. Here we have a similar result in a more contrived but more highly controlled setting. When experiments using quite different methods generate similar conclusions, the validity of the findings is much enhanced.

The generalizability of these communication-net findings may be very low. For example, Snadowsky (1972) indicates that the differences detected by Shaw cease to be important if the communication-net members are allocated a period of time to organize themselves before they start problem-solving. Hence in looking at these findings we must constantly bear in mind that they are the consequences of certain constraints on communication which are no more than weakly analogous to the constraints found in everyday organizations.

Shaw attempts to develop a theoretical explanation of the different properties of various communication-nets. He suggests that the key determinants are the degree of 'independence' which the network provides and the degree to which the network is 'saturated'. We shall examine these concepts in turn. The independence of a network member is the degree to which he is able to solve the problem without depending on the actions of others. Thus all network members are at least partially dependent on others. In a wheel network the central member is much more independent than the others, whereas in a circle all members are equal in being moderately dependent. Shaw follows Leavitt in proposing that in our culture independence enables a network member to satisfy needs for autonomy, recognition and achievement. Dependence, on the other hand, will prevent satisfaction of these needs. A frustrated network member may not feel like sharing his information with others; it follows therefore that high dependence will affect not only satisfaction but also performance.

Shaw's concept of saturation is proposed in order to account for the finding that on more complex tasks the circle does best. The complex problems were tasks such as constructing sentences and solving arithmetic problems. They were complex in the sense that they require more than the mere collation of information. Saturation occurs when a task imposes demands on a network member greater than he is able to meet. Saturated networks are therefore inefficient ones. Shaw's suggestion is that on the complex tasks the central member becomes so overloaded by incoming messages and the necessary data manipulations required that he is very slow to solve the problem.

The several dozen published research studies using the communication-net method do fit rather well into the suggested framework. Shaw's analysis of the experiments is a *post hoc* one, however, so that further experiments will be required to provide more stringent tests.

Let us examine the implications of the Shaw model for settings in which interaction is more sustained and less focused on a single simple task. The model suggests two ways in which the environment may constrain or limit the behaviour of a group or organization. Firstly, the task may impose such a high level of dependence on members that their individualistic motivations are not satisfied. This may cause them to leave the situation or to perform well below their capability. Secondly, the task may impose on members demands they are unable to meet. This will cause them some stress and may also cause them to leave the situation. They may individually perform at a high level but the performance of the group or organization will be below the potential of the system as a whole. Between these two extremes lies a range of situations in which there is a balance between the demands of the task, the needs of the individuals and the capacities of the individuals.

The manner in which independence and saturation were varied by experimenters in the communication-net studies was by permitting or preventing communication between each of the various potential pairs in the network. The presence or absence of communication links is one of the most potent ways in which the environment constrains social interaction. This is notable in field studies of small groups and even more so in analyses of organizations. The provision or absence of communication links in large organizations is a key aspect of the control exercised by higher management.

Small-group ecology

A small group may be thought of as a type of open communication-net in which all are able to communicate simultaneously with all. Such a conception may be fairly valid within an experimental setting, but it overlooks the importance of the time dimension. Even very long-term groups such as families are not in constant communication with one another. Some members of the group see more of one another than do others. The frequency of these interactions is often dependent on environmental constraints.

Festinger, Schachter and Back (1950) report a study of friendship patterns among graduate students at Massachusetts Institute of Technology. They found that the probability of becoming friendly with someone was an arithmetic function of proximity. Students whose rooms were more inaccessible had less friends, while those who were accessible had more and they tended to be people from near by. This effect is presumably obtained because the nearer one lives to someone the greater the probability that one will meet by chance and therefore the greater the probability that one will begin communicating. Once communication is established, processes of social comparison and control will begin to operate, but the communication link has first to be established. In Chapter II it was indicated that under many conditions people like to engage in social comparison with persons similar to themselves. The M.I.T. graduate student population is likely to be a very homogeneous one, in terms of such variables as age, intelligence and social class. Hence, under these conditions it appears that friendship was largely determined by proximity. However, one should not assume that this will always be the case. Where a population is more heterogeneous, initial communications might be discouraging as each partner discovered how different he was from the other. Under these conditions, proximity would not be a predictor of friendship at all. This is often found in large cities, where friendships arise not out of residential proximity, but out of occasions when people meet others more similar to themselves.

Thus one effect of the environment is that it may prevent certain patterns of communication. If it permits them, this still does not ensure that those patterns will arise, but the prevented patterns are definitely ruled out. The restrictions which environment can place on small-group interaction, even when everyone is placed in the same room, can be considerable. Sommer (1967) has investigated a number of such restrictions. He found that different seating patterns in groups were associated with different types of group atmosphere. Where children were given a competitive task, they chose to sit at right angles at a table. Where they were given a co-operative task, they sat side by side. In studies with students different sections of the same class were experimentally scheduled for rooms with quite different physical layouts. It was found that students participated more in the discussions where a circular layout of chairs was used. Least participation was obtained in a chemistry laboratory setting with a series of parallel benches. Most of the talking in these settings was done by those at the front. In these naturalistic studies there was no control over who sat where, so that we cannot be sure that the effect was due to seating positions rather than to choice of particular positions by those who liked to talk.

Steinzor (1950) showed that in experimental discussion groups people tended to speak in response to those sitting opposite to them. Hearn (1957) showed that where an authority figure was present this trend was reversed, and people tended to speak more to those sitting beside them.

Sommer (1969) has pointed out the enormous practical implications of studies such as these. Although the findings to date are scattered and incomplete, it is clear that decisions customarily taken by architects and interior designers in fact have a marked effect on the social structures which emerge. If the seating in an old people's home is arranged so that people cannot talk to one another, or the noise level in a factory workshop prevents sustained conversation, the emergent social structure is heavily affected by these constraints.

The reason why certain seating patterns in a group are more likely to facilitate communication than others appears to be that one needs to obtain visual as well as verbal feedback from those with whom one is interacting. Given a free choice, participants in groups with an established leader will position themselves at some distance from him but in such a way that they can see him and he can see them. In the classes Sommer conducted in chemistry laboratories, the students who spoke were those who could most easily make eye-contact with the leader. The circular pattern often preferred by more informal groups maximizes the possibility of eye-contact between all members of the group. Seating patterns of furniture within offices often also facilitates or makes more difficult the incidence of eye-contact.

Sayles (1958) undertook a comparative survey of the character of workgroups in a variety of different industrial shop-floor settings. He categorized groups as either 'apathetic', 'erratic', 'conservative' or 'strategic'. Sayles's work is correlational so once more we cannot be sure what causes what, but it is interesting to note the environmental circumstances associated with each type of social structure. Sayles also makes clear that his four types are 'ideal types'; in other words, they represent abstractions by the researcher of trends which he sees in a number of different groups in the field. A group which exactly fits the definition of one type and satisfies none of the criteria for the other types may not exist.

Apathetic groups were reported by Sayles to be found mostly among those doing relatively unskilled, low-paid jobs. The work was often dangerous or unpleasant. Different workers might need to co-operate in order to complete the task, but if so their tasks were complementary rather than similar to one another. Apathetic groups appeared discontented but expressed relatively few grievances. There was frequent disunity and friction and no clearly accepted leaders among the men.

Erratic groups were found where everyone had identical or near identical tasks to perform. The workers in erratic groups also needed to co-operate with one another, but they had much more control over the nature and incidence of co-operation. In apathetic groups the work was often paced by the machines. Here the workers had more control over their machines. Erratic groups tended to have highly centralized leadership; they were easily inflamed but not consistently so. At some times their leadership was implacably opposed to management, but at other times it achieved changes in improved procedures which management themselves were quite unable to achieve.

Strategic groups were doing fairly highly esteemed jobs. The skills required for the work usually involved the exercise of judgement by the worker, in a manner which made time-study difficult. The jobs were also relatively important to the functioning of the factory as a whole. The men who did them often had no likelihood of obtaining further promotion to more desirable jobs. These groups were characterized by a pattern of consistent and well-planned grievances. They were highly cohesive, highly productive and consistently involved in maintaining union activities.

Sayles's final category was the conservative groups. These did the most highly esteemed and most highly rewarded shop-floor tasks. Their work was often individual in nature and they were often spatially widely distributed. They tended to be highly satisfied with the situation as it was and resolved their differences with management with ease and without the use of threats.

The differences identified by Sayles between different shop-floor workgroups are vivid and complex. We have discussed already the manner in which the early picture of the industrial shop-floor workshop provided by the Hawthorne studies must be diversified. Just as Lupton (1963) did, so Sayles explores various possible explanations of the wide variance in the behaviour of the different groups. The fact that some of the groups were much more highly paid than others provides the most obvious reason for differences in behaviour. Sayles suggests that this and a number of other comparative factors between different workgroups determine the amount of grievance experienced by group members. On the other hand, the ways in which these grievances are or are not expressed will be a function of the relationship between the men and the type of work they are engaged in.

In terms of the concepts we have been using in this book, the various work environments will either foster or hinder group formation. This in turn will make easy or difficult the processes of social comparison and of control. Where interaction between individuals is difficult, group formation will be hindered. This appears to be the case with apathetic and conservative groups. These arise in environments where either the workers are widely distributed or they find it difficult to interact because they must attend to the more pressing demands of the machines which pace their work or even threaten to injure them. Where interaction does occur, social comparison can proceed. We have discussed earlier how under most circumstances Person selects a comparison Other similar to himself. It is thus no surprise to find that erratic groups have highly similar work and highly similar economic interests. Such conditions facilitate the development of a strongly held view as to the equity or inequity of a given situation. Equally they facilitate the emergence of consensus as to what type of leadership is most acceptable.

The worker in a strategic group has most to lose. He is relatively well rewarded, but, unlike the members of conservative groups, he is well placed to make continuing comparisons with others. The strategic positioning of his task in the organization enables his leaders to achieve success in bargaining to a marked degree.

Sayles's typology illustrates the manner in which the environment pervasively limits and constrains the culture of shop-floor workgroups. Many other instances are available from other settings. We shall explore instances where groups face stress, and instances within school systems. A number of studies have investigated the effects on groups of operating in exceedingly hostile environments, such as attempting to climb Mount Everest, spending the winter at the South Pole or living three hundred feet under the sea for ten days. Radloff and Helmreich (1968) report a detailed study of the last of these. Groups of nine or ten spent ten days in a 'sealab' on the sea bed, while engaging in a variety of underwater exploration and salvage activities. Radloff and Helmreich report that the very high level of danger to which the men were exposed engendered a high level of cohesion. In general, stress leads members of a group to increase their dependency on the group, accept more direction from the leader and conform more closely to group norms. This may be partly because high stress is also associated with the cutting off of cues from other groups, but it is also in line with Schachter's (1959) ideas about the bases of social comparison.

Another environmental constraint on organizational behaviour is the size of the organization. In a series of studies, the behavioural environments of different sizes of schools in Kansas were compared (Barker and Gump, 1964; Barker, 1968). Comparisons were also made of English and American schools. In general it was found that smaller schools provided greater opportunities for children to participate in group activities. With increasing school size there is a greater likelihood that the child will become 'audience' to many events rather than a participant in them.

The 'technology' of a school differs from that of an industrial organization in that the primary task is not the profitable creation of goods but the facilitation of learning. In the past, influential figures in the British educational system have argued that increased effectiveness of learning processes is achieved by streaming pupils into separate classes by their respective ability levels. The principal argument is that such streaming enables the teacher to attend more closely to the needs of his pupils and hence to generate more effective learning. The system of streaming constitutes a major environmental constraint on the type of group structures which will emerge within different types of schools. A number of case studies have been reported of the effects of this system. For example, Hargreaves (1967) reports on a secondary modern school, while Lacey (1970) studied a grammar school. Both these studies show that the effect of streaming is to highlight the differences between the streams. By selecting similar children to go into the same class, it is ensured that these children will interact primarily with one another, will engage in social comparison with one another and will throw up leaders who are an expression of what they share in common. The academically most favoured streams evolve a structure which accepts the values of the school and strives to attain them. The popular children are the intelligent ones. In the less favoured streams the values of the teachers are rejected and a 'delinquescent' culture evolves (Hargreaves, 1967). The popular children are more likely to be the disturbed or aggressive ones. There are a lot of differences between schools and factories, but none the less one can see some similarities between the academically favoured streams and Sayles's conservative groups and between the delinquescent streams and Sayles's erratic and strategic groups. Just as the production system selected in a particular factory constrains and limits the social structures which emerge, so do the learning systems employed in the schools.

Organizations and their environments

In discussing the interplay between group structures in schools and the educational environment, we have moved from an examination of individual group structures to the more global question of why particular organizations select the production technology or type of learning system that they do. To cite a specific instance, the production line technology of a car firm may facilitate the emergence of erratic workgroups, but what variables determine the fact that that particular technology is adopted?

Most researchers into such questions make use of what can broadly be thought of as a 'systems' approach. That is to say they conceptualize organizations as 'open systems' engaged in a complex interrelation with their environment. An open system imports a variety of resources from its environment, transforms those resources in some way, and then exports the products of this transformation. This cycle is repeated many times over, in such a manner as to preserve the organization from extinction. The materials taken in by an organization include not only men, money and materials but also information on the state of the external environment. This information is used to extend the degree to which the organization can predict and control its environment. A system's adaption to a complex environment often involves a bewildering increase in size and differentiation. Systems theorists have been influenced both by the development of computers and by thinking in biology. They emphasize the multitude of different forces to which an organization is exposed. Their thinking thus contrasts very much with those of the small group experimenters, who normally attempt to control all but a few sources of variance within their experiments. The simplest possible expression of a systems model of an organization is that given in Figure 6 (p. 51).

One tradition of work in this field is that associated with the Tavistock Institute in London. They conceptualize organizations as 'socio-technical' systems, in other words systems which attempt to keep in balance the social and technical demands acting on a situation. Their approach is well illustrated by a series of studies (Trist *et al.*, 1963) investigating changes in the coal-mining industry. The principal pressures generating change in the coal-mining industry over the past few decades have been economic and technological. The development of more mechanized systems of coal extraction has reduced costs. At the same time, the development of alternative sources of energy supply has placed mining under threat. In a study of the Durham coalfield, Trist *et al.* charted the replacement of the 'room and pillar' technology by 'longwall advance'. In the room and pillar system, a small group of men worked autonomously, sharing all the requisite tasks among them and bargaining for their piece-rate payment directly. The system of longwall advance which replaced it split up the component tasks into a number of specified different roles. Coal-getting became a three-phase cycle whereby each successive shift had different tasks to perform. The small-group system was in effect replaced by something analogous to a factory production-line system. The work team became a unit of thirty or forty men, but they were not all present in the pit at the same time. The technological changes presented enormous economic advantages, but the change in the social system of the mine was far from beneficial. Various indices of stress when measured under the new system were much higher and a good deal of conflict developed between the shifts who succeeded one another. The conflicts often centred on work which one shift did not have time to complete, which was thus left for the incoming shift.

In later parts of their book, Trist *et al.* illustrate how the technological changes did not necessarily have to have these detrimental effects on the social system. By abandoning the rigid system of fixed roles and adopting 'composite' working, morale was once more restored. Under composite working each man worked on whatever next needed doing and the team took responsibility for the task as a whole. This research permits two conclusions. The first is reminiscent of the conclusions arising from the communication-net experiments: the environment limits but does not determine social structure. Although some possible social structures are eliminated by the absence of the possibility of certain communication links or interaction, there remains a range of possibilities which can be created by appropriate effort. The second conclusion arising out of the Tavistock work is the usefulness of conceptualizing conflict as part of any model of organization. The socio-technical model emphasizes the manner in which organizations will seek to optimize their adaptation to their environment *as a whole*. If the organization as a whole is well adapted this implies some degree of non-optimality on more specific criteria. Thus the mining industry's need to survive led them to ignore aspects of morale for a time. We shall return to the question of conflict within organizations in more detail in Chapter VI.

Another attempt to relate production technology to organizational structure is the work of Woodward (1965). Woodward made a survey of all firms in the south-east Essex area employing more than one hundred people. She finally obtained data from one hundred such firms. The production technology employed by each firm was then categorized as either 'unit', 'batch', 'line' or 'continuous process'. These assessments of technology were then compared with simple measures of the organizational structures of the firms. Large differences were found. Production-line and continuous process firms were found to have a far higher proportion of employees not directly engaged in production. In production-line firms these people tended to be first-line supervisors, whereas in process firms they were more likely to be specialists. Woodward found that, within a given technology, there was some variation from firm to firm, thus confirming the Tavistock finding that there is still choice in how to organize. But she claimed that the firms whose structures were typical rather than aberrant for a given production technology were consistently the most successful.

This finding, if upheld, could be very important. It suggests an analogue at the organizational level to Fiedler's contingency model. Just as different leaders suit different situations, so do different organizational structures suit different technological environments. Unfortunately, Woodward's study cannot be accepted as conclusive without reservation. She gives rather little detail of how firms were categorized. Since on *a priori* grounds it would seem that most large firms have elements of all four production types within them, it is rather important to know how the codings were done, and whether independent coders would come up with the same answer on different occasions. Furthermore, Woodward's measure of the success of organizations was a single index based on the pooling of various diverse performance criteria. Little detail is given of what went into the index, and none at all of how the criteria were combined. Woodward's study is thus highly provocative but somewhat inconclusive. We saw earlier that Fiedler's criteria for assessing the effectiveness of leaders are open to criticism, but the assessment of organizational effectiveness is an issue on which there is still less agreement. Woodward's measure consequently needs to be justified, rather than assumed to be the most appropriate one.

While the point may not yet be firmly established, it remains highly likely that different environments require different structures. In order to test such propositions more detailed analyses will be required of the types of social relationship which are the most productive on specific tasks. This may be a question which is easier to answer through the use of laboratory experiments than through organizational studies and we shall turn to such experiments in the next chapter.

At the organizational level, one can envisage two possibilities. The first is that performance on a given task is essentially an individual activity. The individual performing it will need to be in communication with relevant others at appropriate times but, for the most part, the processes of social comparison and control constitute distractions or blockages to his effectiveness. Such tasks are termed disjunctive by Thibaut and Kelley (1959). Organizations engaged on disjunctive tasks would require a 'differentiated' structure, which kept component parts separate. An example would be an organization engaged in research or problem-solving, which would need to ensure that the process of developing original ideas was kept separate from the process of evaluating and exploiting them. If this were not done, the flow of novel ideas might dry up.

The second possibility is that, on another kind of task, social comparison and control could enhance the individual's effectiveness. Such tasks are termed conjunctive by Thibaut and Kelley. Organizations engaged on conjunctive tasks would require an 'integrated' structure, in which people's activity is securely linked together. An example would be an organization engaged in psychotherapy or training, such as a therapeutic community or an approved school. Here the main priority is to ensure a clear and consistent understanding of the processes of social comparison and control as they occur, since the goal is to use them for therapeutic effect.

The distinction between differentiated and integrated structures in organizations is due to the work of Lawrence and Lorsch (1967). They envisage a continuum from organizations which are highly integrated to those which are highly differentiated. Differentiated organizations clearly also need some degree of integration or else they would cease to function in a unitary manner. On the other hand, integrated organizations do not require differentiation. The ideas of Lawrence and Lorsch have been considerably influenced by the work of Woodward and of Fiedler which we have already discussed. Lawrence and Lorsch envisage a range of environments which require different organizational structures. Their conception of environment rests not so much on different technologies as on the rate of change. They studied six firms in the American plastics industry, which is subject to a very high rate of market change and in which the various different markets for plastics have quite different parameters. They predicted that effective firms in this environment would need to be both differentiated and effectively integrated. They did indeed find that the two most effective firms were more differentiated and integrated than the other firms. Their measures of effectiveness are more clearly spelled out than Woodward's were. Integration was measured from ratings by those involved of how well departments worked together. Differentiation was measured by the degree to which departments were different from one another on four dimensions: formality of structure, interpersonal relations, time perspectives and the type of work goals they had.

Lawrence and Lorsch next extended their study to two further industries to test the generality of their findings. What they hoped to find was that in less rapidly changing environments the effective firms were not of the same type as were those in plastics. They studied two firms manufacturing standardized containers, for which there is a very stable market, and two further firms in the packaged food industry, in which the market shows some change, but not so much as in plastics. The findings are given in Table 1. It can be seen that the requirements in each industry are different and that in each case the effective firm is closer to them than the ineffective one. These findings give a vivid picture of the manner in which the social processes within organizations do have measurable consequences leading to organizational effectiveness or ineffectiveness. From this level of examining organizational performance as a whole, we now return to small-group studies for a more intensive investigation of why it might be that integration hinders performance on one task but aids performance on another.

Summary

The processes of social comparison and control are enhanced, limited or prevented by the nature of the environment within which particular social interactions occur. This is most obvious in situations in which the environment physically prevents communication, such as the communication-net studies and those linking proximity and acquaintance. Even within face-to-face groups seating position affects frequency and type of communication.

Shop-floor workgroups can be categorized as apathetic, erratic, conservative or strategic, depending on the settings within which groups work. Similarly in schools, informal group structures are heavily influenced by decisions as to whether or not to stream children by ability.

TABLE I *Environmental requirements and organizational structures in three industries**

Industry	*Average required differentiation*	*Average required integration*	*Organization*	*Average differentiation*	*Average integration*
Plastics	10·6	5·4	High performer	10·7	5·6
			Low performer	9·0	5·1
Foods	8·7	5·4	High performer	8·0	5·3
			Low performer	6·5	5·0
Containers	6·3	5·5	High performer	5·7	5·7
			Low performer	5·7	4·8

* Adapted from three tables in *Organization and Environment: Managing Differentiation and Integration* by Paul R. Lawrence & Jay W. Lorsch. Copyright 1967. Used with permission of Harvard Business School. The figures in the table are ratings. For differentiation scores range from 3 to 15. For integration the range is 1 to 7. The measures of required differentiation and integration were derived from ratings by managers within the organizations describing the environments facing the different functions. The measures of actual differentiation and integration were based on ratings by the managers of the way their organizations currently were.

Groups may be conceptualized as open systems, which helps one interpret the interplay of social and technological factors. The Trist *et al.* studies indicated that technological factors may limit social comparison and social control, but they do not determine it entirely. There is still room for choice and for deliberate organizational design. Woodward claimed to have shown that different organizational structures did well under different production technologies, but her measurement methods were weak. Lawrence and Lorsch's study was more securely based. They showed that organizations which had adapted their degree of differentiation and integration to the rate of change in their environment were more successful.

V Social Facilitation

The effects which people have on one another's performance of tasks have been a subject of research for many years. Indeed, one of the very first experimental studies in social psychology was concerned with this problem (Triplett, 1897). Triplett studied the manner in which an individual's performance was enhanced by the presence of others. His thinking was stimulated by considering why cyclists could race faster against one another than against the clock. In studying the problem, he designed experimental tasks such as winding fishing reels and concluded that the presence of others definitely facilitated performance. However, he encouraged his subjects to compete with one another so it is not possible to be too sure what caused the effects he found.

Individual tasks

Allport (1920) extended these studies to a whole range of tasks. In all his studies the tasks were essentially individual, i.e. different people would work side by side on the same task, but without the possibility of helping one another in any way. His instructions were intended to minimize competition between his subjects. Allport found that on some tasks the presence of others did indeed enhance performance, but that on other tasks it inhibited performance. For example, enhanced performance was found on multiplication, vowel cancellation and word association tasks. But decreased performance was found on a test in which one had to disprove the arguments of ancient philosophers. In seeking to explain why these differences are obtained we must return once more to the fundamental group processes delineated in earlier chapters. We saw in Chapter II how people tend to engage in social comparison with others. Presumably the subjects in Allport's experiments were doing this when working with others but were prevented from doing so when working alone. But are there any reasons why social comparison might enhance performance on some tasks and inhibit it on others?

For many years no plausible explanation was available. However, in 1965 Zajonc advanced the generalization that, both in the work of Allport and of others, the tasks on which enhanced performance was found were well-known familiar tasks, whereas those on which decreased performance was found were unfamiliar novel tasks. In terms of social comparison, it is clear that Zajonc's theory is highly plausible. On a familiar task, the subject has little need of social comparison and is easily able to obtain what data he needs from others on how well he is working. The fruits of such comparisons will frequently be confirmatory, which will enhance his performance. On unfamiliar tasks, on the other hand, the subject will find it more and more difficult to engage in social comparison. The less familiar the task, the less clear will it be to him how he can evaluate his success or failure on the task. The less clear the data he gets from others, the stronger will become his need for social comparison. Consequently, his performance will suffer as he devotes an increasing proportion of his time to seeking adequate comparison data. Thus social comparison can both augment and inhibit performance. The familiarity of the task turns out to be a key variable, just as the rate of change proved to be crucial in some of the organizational studies examined in the last chapter. We shall discuss divergences between the experimental studies and organizational ones in a moment, but for the moment let us place the data side by side.

Lawrence and Lorsch (1967) found that in unchanging environments firms with *integrated non-differentiated structures* were most effective. The Zajonc model indicates that familiar tasks are best done *in the presence of others*. Lawrence and Lorsch found that in rapidly changing environments, firms with structures which were at the same time both *highly differentiated and highly integrated* were the most effective. The Zajonc model indicates that new tasks are best done *away from others*.

One should not be carried away by this apparent parallel. For instance, the laboratory studies we have examined so far have been concerned with essentially individual tasks, whereas many organizational tasks require collaboration. Furthermore, the laboratory tasks were carried out with no kind of leadership structure present. Finally the differentiated state of some of the organizations studied by Lawrence and Lorsch should not be seen as implying that in these organizations people worked individually all the time. The differentiation was between organizational units, not between individuals. Within any one organizational unit there is no reason to doubt that social comparison will occur. Within a highly differentiated organization it will presumably occur primarily within units, whereas in a less differentiated organization social comparison might be more widely spread. An individual working totally in isolation and without the possibility of making any kind of social comparisons is unlikely to occur outside the experimental laboratory.

We shall need to consider whether the apparent parallel between Zajonc's model and the organizational findings can be sustained as we consider studies having more in common with real organizations.

Collaborative tasks

Group performance on a wide variety of collaborative tasks has been examined. It may be useful to distinguish those studies which use tasks or problems where there is a clearly defined right answer from those where there is no such answer. The distinction is the same as that made by Fiedler between structured and unstructured tasks. In studies using structured tasks the goal has usually been to determine whether groups or individuals come up with better solutions. Studies using unstructured tasks have focused instead on whether group participation is more persuasive than individual methods in changing attitudes or behaviour. In each of these fields, there has been a progression away from simply asking whether groups or individuals do better and towards formulating theories attempting to explain the findings.

Structured tasks

Researchers using structured tasks have frequently found groups to be superior. However, such superiority needs to be closely examined. If we find that groups are superior to individuals in making a particular type of judgement, this may be only because each group comprises a number of different individuals. By combining the judgements of the individuals, the group judgement is likely to average out the errors in the individual judgements. This effect is not so much a group effect as a statistical effect. In order to study true group effects we need to compare the performance of groups not only with individuals but also with sets of individual data which are pooled by the experimenter into 'pseudo-groups' comprising the same number of individuals as the true groups. The pseudo-groups never meet as people: they exist only in the sense that the experimenter assembles their individual scores together.

Studies in which true groups perform better than pseudo-groups should be those using conjunctive tasks, in which members have a chance to augment one another's behaviour, perhaps by a division of labour or the kind of social facilitation discussed earlier. Studies in which pseudo-groups are better, on the other hand, should be those using disjunctive tasks in which people get in one another's way either through mutually incompatible behaviour or through conformity pressures arising out of social comparison processes.

An example of a conjunctive task is provided by the work of Olson and Davis (1964). They set five separate and self-contained arithmetic problems to individuals and to groups of four people. The groups of four were superior and remained so even after the researchers had compared the groups with a baseline derived from pooling individual performances. An example of the second type is provided by the studies of group creativity. Following the development of 'brainstorming' procedures (Osborn, 1957), Taylor, Berry and Block (1958) attempted to test whether groups were able to come up with more original ideas than were individuals. Under brainstorming procedure groups attempt to create a 'freewheeling' atmosphere where any ideas, however absurd, are recorded. Evaluation of the quality of ideas is strictly excluded and is carried out after the idea-generation phase is complete. Osborn's view is that the flow of ideas in the group will trigger off further ideas whereas the usual evaluative framework will tend to stifle imagination. This may be because group members are concerned not to appear ridiculous in the eyes of others.

Taylor, Berry and Block (1958) tested the efficacy of group brainstorming. They found, as expected, that groups produced more ideas than individuals, that groups produced more unique ideas and that the ideas were of better quality as judged by various criteria. However, when the groups' performance was compared with scores for pseudo-groups constructed by the experimenters from the individual scores, the pattern was reversed. The pseudo-groups were superior to the real groups on all criteria. In other words, the superiority of groups over individuals is simply a product of the greater number of man-hours they take up. Even under brainstorming instructions, the presence of others served to inhibit rather than to enhance creativity in these *ad hoc* groups, although it remains possible that brainstorming might be more effective in more established groups or specially trained ones.

The use of pseudo-group data as a baseline has enabled us to distinguish the Olson and Davis arithmetic task on which true groups were superior from the brainstorming task on which they were not. We should note that this difference is consistent with Zajonc's generalization about groups working on individual tasks. In the studies we have just reviewed, the task on which the group enhanced performance was a routine one, whereas the task on which groups inhibited performance was one requiring novel thinking.

The decision as to whether to use group or individual methods in solving some real world problem will, however, rarely rest solely on which procedure is most productive. There is also the question to consider of what to do with the product. Take for instance the Taylor *et al.* brainstorming findings. If we are in need of ideas as to what problems would arise if one had two thumbs on each hand (one of Taylor's experimental tasks) it would be better to ask four individuals than to ask a group of four. But the four-man group would at least produce a single unified list of ideas. On the other hand the four individuals would produce four separate lists very probably involving considerable overlap. If one wanted a clear answer, further work would be necessary to integrate the four different products. In the experiment this extra work must have been done by the researchers who constructed the pseudo-groups. We are not told anything about how long it took. A more valid comparison of the man-hours involved in group or individual working would include also the time required to integrate individual projects (Collins and Guetzkow, 1964).

Once more, the parallels with Lawrence and Lorsch's findings are apparent. In the plastics industry successful firms were highly differentiated in response to rapid change. But this differentiation created a strong need for integration. Likewise the creativity task is best performed by differentiated individuals, but the individual products then require integration. Whether this process of differentiation followed by integration is worth while will depend on the quality of the environment. In an environment where it is absolutely vital to come up with the best possible solution, it would clearly be worth while. But where any one of a number of new ideas would suffice, or where the labour costs of an intensive search would be disproportionate, or where there is reason to predict that one particular individual is more likely to solve the problem, less elaborate procedures could be used.

In comparing group performance with individual performance we have made use of the 'pseudo-group' baseline. This procedure has built-in psychological assumptions which need to be made explicit. Pseudo-group scores are arrived at simply by adding together the individual scores. The assumption built into this procedure is that if the group were actually to meet, all members would be equally influential in determining the group's solution. However, some of the arguments often heard in favour of group methods are that those with the best ideas will be able to persuade others of their merit, while those whose ideas do not solve the problem will learn from others why their ideas are not adequate. Thus the potential performance of a group should be considerably above the pseudo-group baseline. Davis (1969) reports studies in which the group's performance in solving various problems is compared with various baselines incorporating different assumptions about how a group might make use of its constituent skills. Performance approximated most closely to the 'equalitarian' baseline, in which a score was created based on the assumption that each member of the group obtains an equal say. Performance was consistently below the 'hierarchical' baseline, in which a score was created which was based on the assumption that the members with the best solutions would always persuade their colleagues to adopt it.

These findings are interesting but they probably tell us more about the nature of laboratory experimental groups than they do about the potentialities of groups. Davis's groups were *ad hoc* groups without formally appointed leaders. It is therefore not too surprising that their performance was in line with the equalitarian baseline. More effective leadership structures might have evolved, given greater time. An organizational group faced with a problem would almost always have a leader, and that leader would frequently see his task as being to mobilize group resources to confront the problem. Studies are needed of how successful leaders can be in achieving this task. By focusing on leaderless groups, studies in this field have inevitably emphasized the manner in which social comparison processes may inhibit performance and played down the possible impact of leadership in releasing the group's potentialities.

Unstructured tasks

The tasks so far examined have been those on which it is relatively easy to see whether the problem is solved or not. Even in considering the creativity problems used in brainstorming, it was possible, through the use of judges, to evaluate the ideas the subjects came up with. Many tasks facing groups do not have these qualities. Often a group or an individual is faced with the need to decide what course of action to take when it will not be clear for some time whether the correct decision was taken. In the instance of senior management groups it may not become clear until years later. In Chapter II we discussed the manner in which ambiguity fostered social comparison needs. On unstructured tasks we may expect social comparison processes to become more and more important. Conversely, in line with Fiedler's model we may expect leadership to become a more difficult task. This will be partly because the leader will find it difficult to evaluate whether he is making progress or not, and partly because the group members will be that much less ready to accept the leader's initiatives when they cannot see a direct link between his actions and goal accomplishment. In such a situation there will be strong pressure to use group consensus as a criterion for goal achievement.

RISK-TAKING A great many studies have been reported by experimental social psychologists in recent years into the so-called 'risky-shift' phenomenon. Indeed it has probably been the most popular single research topic in social psychology in the late 1960s. The phenomenon was first discovered by Stoner (1961). His subjects were faced with a questionnaire describing twelve hypothetical situations in which someone had to decide how much risk to take. When Stoner's subjects had chosen how much risk they felt was appropriate, they then discussed each of the twelve problems in turn in a group and reached a group decision on each. It was found that the group's decisions were significantly *more* risky than the average of the individuals' decisions. Undoubtedly, this finding appealed to many because it appeared to contradict the widely held view that groups and committees are inherently conservative. One should pause long before concluding that the Stoner finding achieved any such thing. The main differences between risky-shift experiments and a committee are that risky-shift experiments are conducted with *ad hoc,* leaderless, groups usually about five in size and usually faced with situations which are entirely hypothetical. Committees on the other hand are usually long-lasting, with an established leadership structure, larger and frequently faced with decisions which entail very real risks.

As an experimental phenomenon, the risky-shift has been frequently replicated, although the magnitude of the effect is small and by no means all subjects show it. Its occurrence may not tell us much about risk-taking in real groups, but none the less studies of it can be helpful in elucidating what happens in groups faced with unstructured decisions. In considering what might explain this shift to risk two points in particular should be noted:

(1) Researchers who have used other methods of assessing the degree of risk endorsed by subjects have obtained much less consistent findings. In some studies they find a shift to risk and in others a shift to caution. Apparently there is something about the questionnaire Stoner used which encourages the effect.
(2) Even on the Stoner questionnaire, two of the twelve items have consistently shown a shift to caution after discussion. The overall effect rests on shifts to risk shown by the other ten items.

Kogan and Wallach (1967), who devised the questionnaire which Stoner used, have argued that the risky-shift is an instance of 'responsibility diffusion'. By this they mean that when one joins a group one shares with the others responsibility for events. Consequently, any one group member will feel less cautious than he would when acting individually. Such an hypothesis is an appealing one, but it is also a hard one to express in more specific forms. Certainly, when an individual joins a group he lays himself open to influence by the group, both through social comparison processes and through control effects. But the diffusion of responsibility hypothesis does not make it very clear why such influence should always be in the direction of enhanced risk. *A priori* it would be equally plausible that on entering a group one would be persuaded by others who invoke the values of caution. The responsibility diffusion explanation is not tenable as it stands: it is unable to explain why the effect occurs mostly with the Kogan–Wallach questionnaire, why it occurs for some subjects but not others, and why it is reversed on certain items of that questionnaire.

A more convincing explanation of the effect is provided by the social comparison model which has been emphasized in this book. A social comparison explanation would go as follows: the Kogan–Wallach questionnaire has considerable ambiguity. When the subject first sees it, he finds that it refers to various situations entailing risk and asks him to select an acceptable level of risk using numerical measures of risk, such as a three in ten chance of failure or a five in ten chance, etc. The subject has some image of himself as someone who takes risks or someone who is cautious in particular situations, but he is not used to thinking of risks in terms of numerical probabilities. He makes his choices, but is uncertain of them. When he enters group discussion, he is glad of the chance to compare his scores with those of others. He finds in the group that a rather wide range of scores has been chosen. Supposing our subject is someone who sees himself as averagely risky: he will wish to compare himself with the average group member. On some topics he finds that the average group member is arguing for greater risk, but on other topics he finds him arguing for caution. Consequently he moves towards risk or caution in the group discussion. In a similar manner highly risky and highly cautious subjects will seek out suitable comparison others. We have still to explain why initial choices turn out to be sometimes more risky than that of the subject and sometimes more cautious. The proposed answer to this is that on items that ultimately show a shift to risk the wording emphasizes the worthwhileness of risk-taking, whereas on items that move to caution the wording emphasizes the dangers of risk-taking.

The literature on the risky-shift is now very extensive (Clark, 1971; Dion, Baron and Miller, 1970). All that can be done here is to point to a few studies which provide the basis for the above interpretation. It will be noted that the interpretation makes it clear why the Kogan–Wallach questionnaire is particularly likely to generate the effect. Madaras and Bem (1968) asked their subjects to complete questionnaires describing what they thought someone would be like who took up a risky or a cautious position on each of the Kogan–Wallach questionnaire items. They found that on the items that showed a shift to risk, persons favouring risk were the more favourably perceived. But on the items that showed a shift towards caution, persons favouring caution were the more favourably perceived. Thus, on every item, the direction of the shift was towards the more favourably evaluated person. Wallach and Wing (1968) and various other investigators asked subjects to guess what decisions other individuals would have made, on average *before* they started the group discussion. They found that on items that move to risk, most people perceived themselves as *more* risky than average; but on items that moved to caution they saw themselves as *less* risky than average. Clearly, after the discussion begins, the subjects will discover that they are not more risky than average. Hence they will shift their risk preferences upward on the risk-orientated items and downward on the caution-orientated items.

These studies illustrate the manner in which social comparison processes can be used to account for the findings of risky-shift studies. When one first reads about the effect, it sounds very different from, say, the restrictive productivity norms of the Bank Wiring Observation Room. But on closer examination both phenomena turn out to arise from the process of social comparison. In the field setting of the Bank Wiring group, social comparison reinforces stability, whereas in the experimental setting the initial paucity of information enables group discussion to generate change towards one or other extreme.

As is the case with many studies reported in this chapter, investigators have been little interested in the effects of leadership. A few studies (e.g. Marquis, 1962) have examined the effect of appointing leaders in risky-shift discussions. Little effect was found. At present we know very little about the extent to which leaders can influence the direction and potency of social comparison effects.

INTRODUCING CHANGES A further class of unstructured tasks upon which group performance has been studied have to do with the introduction of changes. Here we are concerned not so much with the quality of the decision a group reaches, but with whether or not they reach a decision they are prepared to accept and to implement. Interest in this question was stimulated by a number of striking field experiments by Lewin and his colleagues during the Second World War (Lewin, 1958). In these studies comparisons were made between lectures and group discussions as methods of persuading housewives to adopt various innovative practices. Group discussion was found to have a much more potent effect. For example, in one study thirty-two per cent of housewives tried out a new meat after discussion, but only three per cent after a lecture. Another classic study in this field is that of Coch and French (1948), who compared different methods of introducing changed working methods among girls working in the Harwood pyjama factory in West Virginia. They found that where girls were transferred individually, they tended to leave; where groups of girls were transferred together they tended to complain and to restrict productivity, but that when group discussions were held with the girls before transfer, they accepted the changes and tended to work at an even higher level than previously.

In terms of the social comparison model, what is presumably happening here is that the introduction of change is potentially threatening and therefore enhances the need for social comparison. The individual methods of change introduction prevent social comparison and are therefore ineffective. The group transfer method permits social comparison but fails to provide any mechanism whereby the girls could discuss their fears about the new system with management. The group discussion method both permits social comparison and provides appropriate leadership through the group discussions. These studies are thus not only studies of the effects of working in groups rather than individually, but also of the effects of participative leadership styles. Indeed, the authors of these studies are closely linked with the Michigan researchers whose model of leadership was examined in Chapter III. In that chapter we concluded that the style of leadership that is most effective varies depending on the situation. We should not, therefore, expect to find that the Coch and French procedure is replicable in all settings. One might find, for example, that in all settings where change is contemplated there exist strong social comparison needs, which can be met by participative discussions; but that in some settings the goals of management and employees are so divergent that management may then be unable to agree new procedures with the employees. In the Coch and French study, conflict was apparently sufficiently low that agreement was possible.

An attempt to replicate the Coch and French study was made by French, Israel and Ås (1960). The study was undertaken in a Norwegian shoe factory. The participation procedures used proved to be no more effective in introducing changes than less participative procedures. The researchers encountered considerable difficulty in winning the co-operation of both management and workers. Management were not wholly behind the experiment and restricted it to more peripheral aspects of the changes; workers for their part were suspicious and did not believe that group methods were a legitimate manner for reaching decisions in their situation. There appear, therefore, to have been three conflicting sets of expectations as to how management should have behaved in this experiment – those of the researchers, those of the workers and those of management themselves. The outcome of this was not so much that participation was tried and did not work, but that it was not fully tested. The attitudes of management and workers in the situation make it likely that it would not have worked even if it had been fully tried.

The failure of the French *et al.* study relative to Coch and French serves as a timely reminder that the determinants of success or failure of such group procedures do not lie solely within the groups themselves. Equally important is the cultural context within which they are undertaken. This includes whatever bases of social comparison and control are customary within a particular community. Hulin and Blood (1968) have reviewed the success of various schemes of 'job enlargement', i.e. attempts to share with the worker a greater degree of responsibility and task variety. They conclude that such schemes are by no means always successful. The most successful attempts appear to be those where the participants are drawn from middle-class occupations or from the rural working class. Urban working-class populations have not responded favourably to job enlargement schemes. Hulin and Blood suggest that middle-class values favour enhanced job involvement while working-class values do not. However, the rural working class, they maintain, are insufficiently numerous to develop a set of values divergent from the middle-class values which dominate their communities. In our terms this would mean that opportunities for social comparison and social control are much greater among the urban working class than among the rural working class. This will result not only in higher levels of unionization but also in a greater degree of consensus as to what is desired in a particular situation.

The studies of participative ways of introducing change have mostly been field studies. This means that it is frequently difficult to be certain just which aspects of a particular situation are crucial to the success or failure of participation. Bennett (1955) attempted to separate out some of the components in a laboratory study. She found that students were more likely to volunteer for experiments where they were required to reach a definite decision and where they perceived that the majority of others were volunteering. No effect was found of persuasion through group discussion rather than through lectures or of making public rather than private commitments. Lowin (1968) suggests that Bennett's discussions may have been rather perfunctory, and it is also clear that the decision subjects were faced with was a good deal more trivial than were those in the field studies. Under these conditions it is possible that subjects were able to obtain all the social comparison data they required without group discussion or public commitment. It will be recalled that, in Schachter's (1959) shock experiments, subjects found that just being with others gave them sufficient data.

One theme of this chapter has been the increased need for social comparison which people have when faced with uncertainty or change. This impairs their ability to work rapidly when with others on some tasks but it renders them more open to influence from other people. This suggests that where people are able to satisfy their social comparison needs, there is a greater potentiality for adaptive social change, at least where such comparison shows the changes to be consistent with their goals. Returning once more to the work of Lawrence and Lorsch, we can hypothesize why the successful plastics firms were the highly differentiated ones. Their success should be due to the fact that in each function of these firms employees were able to make social comparisons with others faced with the same problems. In the light of these comparisons they would be able to work out flexible adaptations to the situations they faced. The adaptations are likely to consist in differentiating or specializing separate activities in response to the varying demands of the environment. By contrast, in the unsuccessful firms, low differentiation would impose on employees social comparison others who are faced with different problems. The consequence of this will be inflexibility and anxiety.

The impetus for the work reviewed in this chapter was initially given by a desire to clarify which type of tasks are most efficiently done by groups and which by individuals. A tentative answer can be formulated to the question: routine tasks and those requiring division of labour are best done collectively, while innovative tasks are better done individually. Where the acceptance of a change is important rather than actually inventing changes, group methods are tentatively indicated. During the years while researchers have come up with these answers, our view of the problem has also changed. Whether to do the task collectively or individually is no longer seen as the main problem: very often, in large organizations, it is inevitable that a problem shall be tackled collectively since its solution affects a large number of different people. The question we might like to pose now is more like: 'What do we know about the properties of groups working on different types of tasks, so that we may devise optimal leadership structures for them?' To this question there are at present less certain answers. The research completed indicates the manner in which social comparison processes mediate group performance on various tasks. But the influence of different leadership styles on these processes is little understood.

The effects of leadership

One series of studies which does shed some light on the potentialities of different leadership approaches is that reported by Maier and Hoffman (1960). They compared the effect of 'developmental discussion' with free discussion on various group decision tasks. Under developmental discussion procedure, the leader establishes a series of sub-goals for the group to achieve in the process of solving problems. Most of the problems used were 'human relations'-type problems. Maier and Hoffman found that leaders trained in developmental discussion were a great deal more successful in obtaining high-quality decisions than were leaders using free discussion. Their definition of a high-quality decision rested on the degree to which the groups based their decision on the facts presented. There is inevitably some scope for argument here, as to whether what researchers consider to be a high-quality decision would appear so also to others. We can conclude that Maier and Hoffman's work certainly illustrates the manner in which leaders trained to use particular approaches can radically modify the product of a group's work.

Bouchard (1969) made a comparison of different styles of group procedure as well as individual work, on a creativity problem. He found, as had others earlier, that individuals were more creative than groups when a pseudo-group baseline was employed. But he also found that groups operating under the brainstorming instructions were significantly more creative than were groups operating under critical problem-solving procedures. The implications of this finding are similar to those drawn from Maier and Hoffman's work. In situations where it is inevitable that a task be done in groups, it is possible to transcend some of the limitations of working in groups by the use of appropriate leadership and procedures.

It is interesting to compare these experimental findings with relevant organizational ones. Pelz and Andrews (1966), who were members of Likert's research group at Michigan, made studies of the management of research laboratories. The organizations studied were doing research and development for the U.S. government. If Bouchard's experimental findings are to be replicated in the field, one should expect to find that the most productive laboratories were those in which the researchers were given as much autonomy from evaluation and administrative detail as practicable. There are of course formidable problems in assessing the quality of performance of a research-based organization. Pelz and Andrews used relatively objective measures such as numbers of publications, which may not always be a valid basis for assessment, as well as more subjective judgements by colleagues. Within the limitations of such measurement procedures, their findings were that productive research laboratories were those in which researchers had both autonomy as to how to proceed *and* frequent communication with supervisors and colleagues. In this way they could stay in touch with the problems on which solutions were needed, without being unduly constrained as to how to tackle the problems. This finding once more calls the work of Lawrence and Lorsch to mind. Effective research supervision appears to occur where there is high differentiation (permissive supervision enables the researcher to have high control over the direction of his research) coupled with high integration (the supervisor and others stay in frequent contact).

We have now examined the manner in which the interaction between environment and social process dictates that certain tasks are best performed by differentiated structures. The work of Pelz and Andrews indicates that the procedure for creating the appropriate blend of differentiation and integration may be far from simple. Creating differentiation is perhaps the simpler part of the equation; groups and organizations are abundantly provided with bases for schism and separation. The problem is to ensure the occurrence of the desired bases of differentiation rather than other ones, and to create ways of integrating this diversity. In the next chapter we turn primarily to the question of relations between groups. Problems of integration exist also within particular groups, but they are most clearly seen in inter-group relations.

Summary

The presence of others may enhance performance if one is engaged on a familiar task, or it may hinder performance if the task is novel. In comparing the performance of groups and individuals one should hold constant the man-hours involved and not forget to take account of the cost of integrating differentiated products. When this is done it is clear that groups do best on routine tasks and where a division of labour is possible. Individuals do best where novelty or creativity is at a premium.

In groups with unstructured tasks, social processes become more salient. Where people are uncertain they may follow the real or perceived group consensus. They may be more willing to accept changes if these changes are in their interests, but less so if they are not.

Often there is little choice as to whether a task is done collectively or individually. It is therefore more fruitful to examine how leaders can make the best of the circumstances they are faced with. There is some evidence that by encouraging the group to adopt procedures appropriate to their task a leader can enhance performance.

VI The Problem of Integration

In analysing the process of social comparison in groups, considerable emphasis was laid on the manner in which people frequently choose social comparison objects rather similar to themselves. The essence of most organizations is that they are large and diverse. Employees differ considerably in age, seniority, skills, social class, interests and sometimes even language. Inevitably a large organization therefore comprises a large number of separate foci of social comparison, with some degree of incompatibility between them. In earlier chapters we have already considered Likert's proposal that managers should be conceived of as linking pins between the different component sub-groups, and we have also reported the manner in which some organizations become more markedly differentiated than do others. In all organizations the problem of integration looms large. The problem does not arise out of personal idiosyncrasies or particular unco-operative individuals: it arises out of the process of social comparison and the development of group loyalties which derives from it.

The incidence of conflict

Let us start by examining the nature of the problem. Gross, Mason and McEachern (1958) made a study of school superintendents in the state of Massachusetts. A superintendent is someone responsible for the schools of a particular district, rather than for one individual school. Gross *et al.* were interested in examining the role of school superintendents. They found that it was not possible to describe the 'role' of school superintendents, if by role one means an agreed set of prescriptions as to how superintendents should behave. They found it more useful to think in terms of the expectations of all those people who seek to influence the manner in which the role occupant behaves. For school superintendents this included school principals, the school board, parent–teacher associations, individual teachers, local community figures, secretaries and so forth. Many of these people had quite different ideas as to how they would like the superintendent to behave. Superintendents could not therefore behave on the basis of some general consensus as to how they should behave. On the contrary, they had to decide how to accommodate seemingly irreconcilable pressures on them to behave in opposite ways. Gross *et al.* report that their 105 superintendents experienced conflicting demands from different people very frequently on the four issues they studied in detail:

53 per cent experienced conflict over time allocation
71 per cent experienced conflict over personnel hiring and promotion
88 per cent experienced conflict over teacher salary recommendations
91 per cent experienced conflict over budget recommendations.

The skill with which the superintendents handled these and other conflicts would be a main component of their effectiveness as superintendents. In terms of the concepts developed earlier, the superintendents were acting as linking pins, or they were engaged in the process of organizational integration. Gross *et al.* analysed how the superintendents went about achieving this. They found it possible to classify the superintendents' orientations along a scale from 'moral' to 'expedient'. When faced with conflict on a particular issue, the moral superintendents would rely on the application of some appropriate universal principle. This could be used in explaining to those whose demands were rejected why it was necessary to do so. At the other extreme were the expedient superintendents, who would weigh up the relative power of the different groups pressuring them and propose a compromise in the light of this. Many superintendents behaved in a manner intermediate between these extreme positions.

Gross *et al.* selected a single rather specialized role for study. It is important to know whether their findings are likely to be applicable to a broad range of roles or not. Kahn *et al.* (1964) conducted studies designed to clarify this point. In the first part of their study, they surveyed a representative sample of the employed U.S. workforce. It was found that a high proportion of the 725 people surveyed reported both conflict between the demands made on them by different people, and also ambiguity and tension concerning what some of the demands actually were. A more detailed study was made of the role problems of fifty-three industrial managers. Conflicting demands were found to occur more frequently at more senior levels within the organization, and among those whose jobs required them to cross organizational boundaries. This applied both to those who crossed boundaries between one department and another, and also to those whose task it was to go outside the organization and make contact with customers, suppliers or clients. These findings make it clear that it need be no surprise that school superintendents experience a great deal of role conflict. Their positions are senior and they are involved in a great deal of boundary crossing.

Kahn *et al.* were also interested in how their fifty-three managers resolved the conflicts facing them. Their analysis is both complex and valuable. One crucial finding is that the conflicts were frequently not resolved at all. If the parties in conflict were not strongly dependent on one another, they often found it less painful to avoid the conflict rather than to resolve it. Only where failure to resolve the conflict had an immediate and obvious effect on the role occupants' ability to perform effectively was there sufficient incentive to confront the conflict. Conflict avoidance may frequently reduce the effectiveness of the organization, but it is not often easy to assess these effects in a concrete manner. On the other hand, conflict avoidance can often have at least short-run advantages to the individual. Kahn *et al.* found that managers who were more than averagely neurotic, introverted or flexible were more prone to stress, and therefore more likely to avoid conflict. In the long run avoidance often serves to exacerbate the situation. By reducing communication relevant to the conflict the parties ensure that their positions will become more differentiated and the problem of integration more acute.

Kahn *et al.* found that attempts to resolve conflicts differed depending on the organizational relationship between the parties. Where one party was the organizational superior of the other, the resolution was likely to be rules-orientated, i.e. it would rest on the right of one party to instruct the other what to do. This resolution procedure is presumably similar to what Gross *et al.* called 'moral' solutions. On the other hand, where conflicts were between those not having authority over one another, greater recourse was made to friendship appeals and to technical expertise. In such situations, 'expedient' conflict resolutions will be more to the fore. Conflict resolution within an authority relationship has been examined earlier, in Chapter III, where a start was made at indicating the settings under which particular leadership styles will be more or less effective. In the present chapter, the focus is more on conflict resolution in situations where authority does not prescribe conflict resolution procedures. Such situations are relationships between organizational colleagues, or between departments, or between autonomous organizations who are none the less interdependent, such as management and unions. Such conflicts are perhaps at their most bitter and sustained when each party engages in social comparison with some professional or class-based comparison group. The classic instance in industrial organizations is staff-line conflict, where a specialist and a general manager are in conflict (Dalton, 1959). The general manager identifies with the organization, while the specialist compares himself with other members of his professional discipline and declines to accept the authority of the line manager. Subordinates are faced with the impossibility of choosing between the specialist's expertise and the manager's authority. In penal institutions there are frequent conflicts between those identifying with groups having custodial or punitive aims and those having therapeutic aims (Zald, 1962). In hospitals, exceedingly complex multiple conflicts may occur with doctors, nurses, administrators, social workers, occupational therapists, psychologists and others each maintaining separate and conflicting identifications with professional reference groups. The recent reorganization of the social services in Britain has also highlighted similar conflicts. Such complexity does not make it easy for the researcher, particularly if he wishes to use experimental methods.

The development of intergroup conflict within naturalistic field experiments has been vividly demonstrated by Sherif (1967). He conducted a series of summer camps for teenage boys. The boys were assigned to two different groups, and kept separate for a few days. The development of a competitive relationship between the two groups was fostered by the use of competitive games. When a hostile relationship between the groups was firmly established, Sherif tested various conflict resolution procedures. His theory was that simple communication between the parties would serve to enhance rather than reduce conflict, since by now each group judged its own success by the failure or humiliation of the other. In effect each group engages in social comparison with the other and contrasts the virtues of itself with the failings of the other. Sherif postulated that this conflict could only be resolved where the goal structure of the situation is modified. Where 'superordinate' goals emerge, which require collaborative effort for their achievement, the divergent, competitive goals will become less salient. Examples of superordinate goals provided by Sherif in his camps were the breakdown of the camp water-supply, which required collective search for the fault; and the breakdown of a lorry used for excursions, which required all to pull on the same rope to get it restarted. Where a series of such superordinate goals were introduced, conflict progressively reduced and the two groups began to integrate.

Sherif's model of conflict has the virtue of clarity. Within this framework, one can presume that Gross *et al.*'s superintendents were making use of one or other possible superordinate goal, appealing either to widely shared moral values such as those favouring fairness or equity, or to the expedient goal of achieving some kind of agreement in order to keep the school system running. Such an analysis is plausible, but since it is entirely *post hoc,* it does not really test Sherif's ideas. Likewise, if one re-examines the Kahn *et al.* findings that many conflicts are not resolved at all, this may be interpreted as showing either that sufficiently compelling superordinate goals were unavailable or, more likely, that no one was present to argue for their relevance. After all, Sherif's groups of boys did not resolve their conflicts by themselves; it required the determined intervention of a third party, namely the powerful experimenter, Sherif himself.

There exists in all the research so far referred to in this chapter a strong implication that conflict resolution is a positive value. Conflict is viewed as a widely distributed phenomenon, but one which the organization must seek to reduce, resolve, integrate or manage. Such a position implies that the overall effectiveness of the organization should always prevail over the individuals or subgroups who comprise it. For example, Kahn *et al.* are critical of conflict avoidance. Such conflict avoidance does very likely limit the effectiveness of organizations, but equally it may preserve the autonomy or mental health of those who are stressed by such conflict. Students of conflict and integration might be better advised to study *both* the effectiveness of methods of achieving organizational integration where this is desired by both parties, *and* the effectiveness of methods of bargaining in situations where goals are permanently in conflict and integration is not desired by both parties. Both types of settings occur frequently in contemporary society.

Effective bargaining procedures

Many laboratory studies have been completed of the effectiveness of different bargaining procedures or strategies. In these, experimental subjects usually bargain on the basis of a simple pay-off matrix with another individual. One frequent format has been the 'prisoner's dilemma' matrix. This provides the individual with an apparent conflict as to whether he shall seek to prosper at the expense of the other party, or whether he shall seek to develop a collaborative relation with the other. The matrix is so constructed that if both parties seek to prosper at the expense of the other, both lose. This can be seen in Table 2. If Player 1 chooses B and Player 2 chooses D, they both achieve a negative outcome. Thus the only viable long-term strategy within this particular matrix is to establish collaboration with the other player. However, this turns out to be exceedingly difficult. One reason for this is probably the fact that in the short run, the only way a player can defend himself against being exploited by the other is to play the non-collaborative choice. Once a pattern of non-collaboration is established it is hard to break, since it requires a co-ordinated decision by both parties to do so.

TABLE 2 *A typical 'prisoner's dilemma' matrix*

		Player 1 chooses between: A	or B
Player 2 chooses between:	C	+5/+5	−10/+10
	or		
	D	+10/−10	−5/−5

NOTES:

(1) Within each cell the left-hand number gives the pay-off due to Player 2; the right-hand number gives the pay-off due to Player 1.

(2) The esoteric title for this matrix refers to an apocryphal situation in which two criminal suspects are said to have been held in isolation from one another. Each was told that if he confessed he would go free, while if he did not there was only sufficient evidence for him to be imprisoned on a minor charge.

However, if both suspects confessed then both would be liable to the heavy sentence, although the prosecution would ask for leniency. This yields a matrix of gaol sentences as shown below. The suspect has the dilemma of whether to settle for 1 year's imprisonment or to risk 8 years' by attempting to get off scot free. He also has to assess the risk that the other suspect may confess, leaving him in prison for the full ten years:

		Prisoner 1: Not Confess	Confess
Prisoner 2:	Not Confess	1yr/1yr	10yrs/free
	Confess	free/10yrs	8yrs/8yrs

Experimental studies using the prisoner's dilemma matrix have almost invariably shown substantial proportions of subjects who fail to establish co-operation (Nemeth, 1970), despite the clear advantage in doing so. This need not challenge our conception of experimental subjects as rational problem-solvers, but it does give occasion to reflect on the nature of the environment in which the studies have been done. Most usually subjects have not been rewarded for their achievements by the payment of real money, but only by the accumulation of notional 'points'. They have only been able to communicate with their fellow-bargainers by note, and are required to make decisions on a particular trial of the experiment in ignorance of what the other party is deciding. Under such circumstances one might expect that the bargainers would be bored and that they might play in such a manner as to maximize interest, rather than invest much effort in the difficult task of establishing a collaboration whose only pay-off would be a boringly uniform accumulation of notional points. In Sherif's terms one would say that the superordinate goal was not very compelling, while the rewards of continued non-co-operation or erratic behaviour were often greater.

Within this context we may turn to those prisoner's dilemma studies which focus specifically on the most effective bargaining strategies. Harford and Solomon (1969) contrasted the effect of 'lapsed saint' and 'reformed sinner' strategies. In each case the subject thought he was bargaining with another person, but actually he was playing against a pre-programmed schedule determined by the experimenter. Under the lapsed saint programme, the subject found his adversary unconditionally co-operative on the first three decisions. Thereafter, the adversary was conditionally co-operative. That is to say if the subject co-operated on a given trial, his adversary reciprocated on the next trial. Likewise, if the subject did not co-operate on a trial, the adversary would retaliate on the following trial. The reformed sinner, on the other hand, was unconditionally unco-operative on the first three trials, and thereafter conditionally co-operative. Thus, although the experiment lasted for thirty trials, the only differences between the lapsed saint and the reformed sinner was on the first three of those trials. It was found that the reformed sinner consistently elicited more co-operation than did the lapsed saint. In this setting apparently, effective bargaining requires that one establish early on that one has the capacity to be non-co-operative if need be. Deutsch *et al.* (1967) obtained a very similar finding with a wider range of subjects and a more naturalistic experimental design. In a similar vein are a series of experiments by Thibaut (1968). In these, an attempt was made to specify the conditions under which the parties would make use of an opportunity to reach contracts limiting various bargaining strategies. It was found that contracts were most frequent where there was a high conflict of interest and where each party was relatively able to withdraw from bargaining altogether if need be.

Another variable relevant to the establishment of co-operation is trust formation. Swinth (1967) postulated that trust would arise in a prisoner's dilemma matrix where one party made himself vulnerable to the other's exploitation and the other responded by *not* exploiting him. This was found to be so. The studies discussed of effective bargaining in experiments imply a bargainer who both emphasizes his strengths and, at an appropriate moment, reveals his weaknesses. However, the studies tell us nothing about the timing of these actions, and skill in bargaining may often be a question of timing.

A somewhat different approach to the study of bargaining is that of Christie and Geis (1970). They investigated the proposition that 'machiavellians' are more adept at achieving their goals in interactive situations than are others. Many of the situations they studied involved bargaining. Machiavellians are those who take a relatively cynical view of human nature and attempt to control the behaviour of others through manipulation and deceit. An early finding was that, as had been believed for many hundreds of years, machiavellians really are more able to look one straight in the eye while telling a lie (Exline *et al.*, 1970).

One study reported by Christie and Geis involved groups of three subjects who bargained for ten dollars. The ground rules were that any two of the three subjects could have the money, so long as they could agree the distribution of it between them. Splitting the money between all three subjects was not permitted. Each triad contained one subject scoring high on machiavellianism, one scoring medium and one scoring low. Seven triads were tested and on every single occasion the high machiavellian got the best of the bargain. Unlike the prisoner's dilemma, this situation is one of irreconcilable conflict. The machiavellians appeared to win by taking control of the discussion and by suppressing any concern with morality or fairness.

In another study, by Christie, Gergen and Marlowe, a prisoner's dilemma matrix was used. Halfway through the experiment the notional stakes were replaced by substantial real money stakes. It was found that the high machiavellians subsequently became more co-operative, while others did not change their strategy. When money is at stake reducing boredom is less of a problem and the rational strategy is more certainly co-operation, so once more the machiavellians were doing the right thing. In a third study (Geis, Weinheimer and Berger, 1970), a complex role-playing design was used. The role-play simulated decision-making and lobbying procedures in Congress. Seven-man groups were used and this time it turned out that machiavellians were also more effective lobbyists.

Christie and Geis's hypothesis is that machiavellians have less need of social comparison and are therefore less distracted by irrelevant affect in bargaining situations. They are more able to see clearly where their advantage lies in a particular situation and to focus more exclusively upon it. This leads them to be sometimes co-operative and sometimes ruthless, depending on the situation. Their success frequently rests on the opportunistic concealment of particular facts. In assessing the importance of these laboratory studies one must ask whether they parallel organizational settings or not. The temporary nature of laboratory experiments obviously favour the machiavellian: he does not have time to be found out. On the other hand, the diffuse contacts of large organizations also provide much scope for concealment. It seems very likely that machiavellians do achieve considerable success as bargainers in large organizations. In time a machiavellian's deceptions may become known, but by the time they have, he may well have been promoted on the strength of earlier achievements.

The findings concerning the effectiveness of machiavellian behaviour are striking and perhaps need to be put into some perspective. What has been found is that in certain settings machiavellians are the most effective at serving their own interests. In other settings they are not. For example, Wallston (1972) found machiavellians to be no better at extracting information from others than were non-machiavellians, in a situation where there were reasons to be suspicious of the machiavellians. No study has shown that an organization run on machiavellian lines is most effective. Machiavellian procedures for organizational conflict resolution are no doubt widespread – one is reminded of Gross *et al.*'s 'expedient' superintendents – but it remains to be shown whether such strategies benefit anyone other than the machiavellian, and those who depend on him.

This section was introduced on the basis that, in certain circumstances, the individual or group may find it right to stand out against integration within the larger organization. It provides some indications as to which courses of action are likely to advance that goal. In time, it may be possible to develop a model of bargaining effectiveness analogous to the Fiedler leadership effectiveness model. In other circumstances organizational integration rather than divergent bargaining may be preferred, and we turn now to this possibility.

Integrative procedures

The strongest force towards integration among colleagues in many organizations is provided by the superordinate goal of resisting the unreasonable demands of higher authority. Unacceptable pressure from above may easily produce a hierarchical system of integrated coalitions (Caplow, 1968) rather than Likert's model of linking pins extending both vertically and horizontally throughout the organization. Such an organization is not an integrated organization, but rather a series of highly cohesive or integrated groups, within a non-integrated organization. This recalls the Seashore (1954) study which showed that cohesive groups had much more uniform productivity than non-cohesive groups. Productivity was uniformly low where the groups were in conflict with management and uniformly high where they were not.

Lawrence and Lorsch (1967) paid considerable attention to the process of organizational integration. In their study in the plastics industry, they found that the integrating procedures used by the successful firms differed in a number of significant ways from those used by the less successful firms. The plastics firms had a considerable need of integration since their structures were strongly differentiated in response to their varied and changing environment. In addition to integrating procedures found in most organizations, such as the use of the hierarchy to resolve disputes and standardized paperwork procedures, the firms also had one or more cross-functional liaison teams as well as a separate department whose prime task was the achievement of integration between the different aspects of the organization.

The successful plastics firms were found to differ from the less successful ones in six respects. Firstly, the integrating department was intermediate in structure between the other departments whose efforts it sought to integrate. In less successful organizations it tended to be more similar to one or other of these departments, and was consequently more likely to be seen as partisan in disputes which arose. Secondly, the integrators' power was seen as resting on technical expertise, rather than stemming from the integrators' senior position in the hierarchy. Thirdly, the integrators in the successful firms felt that their own achievement of rewards or advancement was contingent on achieving integration, while those in the less successful firms did not. Fourthly, managers in the successful organizations felt that they had more influence in general than did those in the unsuccessful organizations. Fifthly, in the successful firms there was a closer match between the levels at which information was available and the level at which relevant disputes were resolved. Finally, in the successful firms there was a greater tendency for conflicts to be resolved through the constructive confrontation of differences, rather than through smoothing things over or through one party forcing a solution on the other.

The picture of organizational integration procedures portrayed by Lawrence and Lorsch is a plausible one. One way of summarizing their findings would be to say that the successful firms had been more effective in establishing integration as a superordinate goal. This was achieved through appointing skilled and senior men to the task and rewarding them for success. This also required close attention to where and how particular decisions should be taken within the organization. Unfortunately the clarity of Lawrence and Lorsch's findings must be qualified by referring back to some of the problems explored in discussing Likert's theory. Lawrence and Lorsch's data, like most of Likert's, is correlational. In other words, although Lawrence and Lorsch have shown that the successful firms differ from the unsuccessful ones, we cannot infer from this that they are successful *because* of their different integration procedures. It would be no less plausible to argue that because certain firms experienced success, they respected their integrators' competence more, felt more influential and confronted their differences in a more open manner. As in the case of the leadership studies the most crucial test is that of experiment. If it can be shown that when the integration procedures of an organization are changed in the directions implied by Lawrence and Lorsch it becomes more successful, then indeed there will be firm evidence that these procedures are causes rather than consequences of success. Such attempts to modify organizational structures will be explored in the final chapter.

One aspect of Lawrence and Lorsch's description of effective integration procedures was the manner in which integrators were able to play a third-party role in resolving disputes. The significance of third parties in conflict resolution of all kinds is considerable and we turn now to an examination of the role of third parties. If two parties in dispute over some issue agree to accord some third party the right to intervene in their relationship, they have already established a superordinate goal. That is to say that by their action they have consented to the proposition that their relationship is worth improving and that something of value will be achieved if it is improved. Of course the two parties will frequently retain considerable misgivings about the potency of the superordinate goal in comparison to their individual goals.

Most attempts to introduce change systematically into groups or organizations involve the use of third parties. In that sense, we shall be concerned with the activities of third parties for the remainder of this book. In this chapter the focus will be more on a consideration of why third parties may be particularly useful in conflict resolution or change induction. It was pointed out earlier that Sherif took an active part in presenting superordinate goals to his groups of boys, i.e. he performed a third-party role. Blake and Mouton (1961, 1965) obtained further comparative data on the effectiveness of various widely used conflict resolution procedures. They established conflict between groups of managers on training programmes. This was achieved by asking each group to produce the best plan as to how time should be spent at a later stage in the training. Various procedures for resolving these conflicts were tested comparatively. Public bargaining between group representatives frequently led to deadlock, while private bargaining was little more effective. Evaluation by neutral third-party judges was seen as fair by those who won and unfair by those who lost. Strong perceptual distortions were noted, whereby each group perceived less in common with the others' proposals than there actually was. Conflict resolution procedures where more effort is put into building the legitimacy of third-party intervention were favoured. For example, a third-party might be selected according to the ground rule that only someone strongly favoured by both parties would be used.

It has already been suggested that the process of social comparison lies at the root of intergroup conflict. Since each group compares itself negatively with the other it becomes very difficult for negotiators or others to give ground to the other party without being seen as traitors. The basis of third-party intervention lies not in social comparison but in control. If a third party is accorded the *right* to influence the parties, this must be because the superordinate goal which he represents outweighs the potency of intragroup social comparison processes. In early chapters we have already noted some instances where control may outweigh social comparison and some where the reverse is true. For example, in Milgram's experiment the group successfully resisted the leader but in the Helmreich and Collins experiment subjects preferred to wait with a leader than with a leaderless group. The third party's task must always be to enhance his legitimacy as an influence agent. This is a perilously difficult task, and most third parties are more powerless than powerful. The integrating departments in Lawrence and Lorsch's study were powerful, but even here their effectiveness apparently rested on their expertise rather than their formal power.

Walton (1969) provides an analysis of procedures used in developing the legitimacy of third-party roles in conflict settings. These include demonstrating high expertise but low formal power, providing neutral settings and sufficient time, establishing good relations with both parties, 'refereeing' discussion, summarizing and clarifying points at issue and diagnosing possible reasons for difficulties encountered.

Conflict within organizations spans a very broad range. Some of the instances of role conflict identified early in the chapter are most frequently handled by being ignored; other conflicts are so damaging and severe that they require third-party intervention in order to achieve any integration at all. In yet other conflicts the bargainer best serves his interest by resisting integration. The dilemma of organizational life is to identify which these last conflicts are: parties to conflicts very frequently believe that by resisting co-operation they are best serving their interests and yet this is not always so. Only where collaboration based on trust is firmly established between parties is it possible to know what are in fact the pay-offs of collaborative organization in that particular setting.

Summary and a suggestion for a practical exercise

Conflict and disagreement are a normal rather than an exceptional component of groups and organizations. They may be resolved by reference to some abstract set of rules or principles, or else on the basis of expediency. Frequently they are not resolved at all but ignored. They are most acute among those in senior positions and whose task it is to cross organizational boundaries.

Conflict resolution frequently depends on the availability of suitable superordinate goals. It occurs most readily where there are opportunities for testing the gradual increase of trust between the parties in conflict. This occurs where each party is able to show both his strength and his willingness to render himself vulnerable.

Successful bargaining in irreconcilable conflicts depends on the converse of these points, a ruthless eye for the main goal one is seeking, the ability to define as irrelevant social relationships and feelings which stand in one's way, and the concealment of one's weaknesses.

Organizational integration is usually achieved by the creation or introduction of powerful and respected third parties and by the use of hierarchical control. The research to date does not tell us whether effective integration of organizations such as those studied by Lawrence and Lorsch is cause or result of organizational success.

This chapter completes that part of the book devoted to an analysis of group and organizational behaviour. From this point on we shall be concerned with attempts to introduce changes rather than to analyse existing situations. As an exercise in rendering more concrete the analytic concepts used in this book, the reader is invited to make an examination of one or more groups to which he belongs. Try to consider these points:

Who compares their behaviour to whom?
How is the control function exercised?
In what manner does the environment constrain the group's structure or performance?
How effectively does the group perform its task(s)?
How does the group relate to other groups?

The same exercise may be undertaken for organizations, but can become unduly complex with increasing size. Such analyses of groups or organizations frequently suggest ways in which changes might be desired. In such a way can diagnosis lead into planning for change.

VII Using Temporary Systems to Change Behaviour

In the first six chapters of this book an analysis has been presented of group and organizational behaviour. The reader may by now feel somewhat more able to look at groups or organizations and to consider which of their qualities are explicable in terms of social comparison processes or of control processes. More likely, the information imparted in these chapters feels somewhat abstract and difficult to apply. Some emphasis was laid in the first chapter on the difficulties which the social sciences face in applying their findings to the solution of real problems. The difficulty is this: the preceding chapters may help the reader to *analyse* group or organizational behaviour, but a cogent analysis (even if this book were to achieve it) is not enough. In order to affect the outcome of real problems, the practical skills of intervening in and influencing those problem situations are required.

We have seen that, in order for groups and organizations to achieve their goals, certain behaviours and structures are required, which differ depending on the situation. This chapter examines attempts to increase an individual's ability to provide the appropriate skilled *behaviour* when a situation requires it. The final chapter will be more concerned with attempts to modify organizational *structures* to make them more appropriate to their task or setting.

One viewpoint on the provision of skills is that of Fiedler (1967). Fiedler believes that the significance of his research into leadership is that it will enable the selection of leaders appropriate to each setting. According to this view training will be unnecessary, since through selection a good match will be obtained between each setting and the required type of leadership. This viewpoint is a hard one to sustain. The crudity of present selection devices makes such a procedure decidedly fallible. More importantly, most leadership settings pose different requirements at different times, so that the leader's ability to provide a range of leadership behaviours will be at a premium. Particularly in rapid change settings it is therefore more likely to be fruitful to train for flexibility rather than to select and assume inflexibility.

The best setting within which to increase an individual's interactive skills is within specially convened small temporary groups. Research into the learning of human skills has repeatedly shown that learning occurs where the individual has an opportunity to practise the skill and to receive feedback as to how effectively he is doing it. Groups assembled for this purpose are usually known as T-groups and the process which occurs in them is known as sensitivity training. The term 'T-group' stands simply for 'training' group. Such groups are typically set up with a very open agenda and plenty of time available for interaction. Under these conditions each member of the group has an opportunity to behave in characteristic ways and to try out some new behaviours as well. Other members of the group will react, thereby providing the feedback necessary for learning.

T-groups

T-groups represent one of the principal social inventions to date which derive from the findings of social psychology. Indeed, their origins can be traced back to the influence of Kurt Lewin (Benne, 1964) who was influential in triggering many of the other key developments in social psychology in the late 1940s. The conduct of T-groups has evolved considerably over the years, but their central features are readily explicable in terms of the concepts used in this book. A T-group typically comprises between eight and a dozen members plus one or two leaders. It meets for anything up to ten days, preferably at a residential setting away from one's workplace. The leader exerts some control over the proceedings, by proposing starting and finishing times for meetings, by expressing his interest in group members and their relationships with one another, and by occasionally proposing specific exercises or activities. But for the most part the leader's behaviour is a good deal less controlling than is that of leaders in other settings. This is because he wishes the members of the group to take responsibility for their own behaviour. In a general sense the goal of the T-group is for each member to increase his skills of diagnosing what goes on in interpersonal relationships and to increase his ability to provide behaviours appropriate to the situation he has diagnosed.

Such broadly defined goals do not initially appear to be much use to T-group members. They find themselves sitting among a group of whom the others are strangers and the leader is apparently unwilling to tell them what to spend their time talking about. Such a situation can be embarrassing or alarming, and the vacuum in the group is soon filled by a variety of behaviours. The isolation of the T-group makes it likely that social comparison processes will be focused within the group, or possibly orientated towards other T-groups undergoing the same programme. The availability of external sources of social comparison is minimized. At the same time, the controlling demands of the everyday environment are also held at bay. The sole representative of external authority in the group is the leader, and he uses his position to focus attention within the group, not away from it. The evolving culture of a T-group thus arises from its rather special circumstances. We shall discuss presently problems of relating this culture to more long-term organizational life, but for the moment let us examine what tends to happen in T-groups.

The initial climate of the group is cautious and anxious. Members introduce themselves to one another and often speak about their jobs more than about themselves. The conversation tends to be disjointed and uneasy. People keep a good deal of their reactions to what is occurring to themselves. In later sessions the group starts to develop a more trusting climate. The fragmented quality of everyday life makes it easy for many of us to preserve the belief that our reactions to life are particularly unique. As members of the T-group start to share with one another their reactions to events in the group, they frequently find that others are surprisingly similar. They too are faced with rather similar fears, strengths, aspirations and frustrations in relating to others. Social comparison within the group thus often leads to confirmation rather than disconfirmation. This in turn strengthens the group's wish to explore further their interrelations with one another. Other comparisons will lead to disconfirmation. A member may find that while he perceived his behaviour towards another as helpful others perceived it as patronizing. There are a number of ways he could respond to this disconfirmation, such as changing his behaviour, changing his perception of those who see him as patronizing, sharing more of his own feelings with his perceivers in an attempt to change their perceptions, etc. If the group member has uniformly experienced disconfirmation in the group, he is more likely to dismiss the others as a credible source of feedback. On the other hand, if he has found that on other issues their perceptions have tended to confirm his own, he is much more likely to 'learn' from the interchange. Thus the successful T-group develops a climate in which both confirmation and disconfirmation play a part. The totally disconfirming group will never command its members' involvement. The totally confirming group will become warm and cohesive, but will generate little impetus for change or learning in its membership.

The task of the T-group leader will be to encourage both of these two processes within the group. This may amount to encouraging others to express their reactions to one another, or to expressing his own reactions where these are relevant. Alternatively, he may provide some analysis of processes within the group in an attempt to clarify why the group is developing in a particular manner. For example, he might suggest that the reason why members appeared not to be listening to one another's comments at a particular time was because the group was engaged in a struggle to determine who should occupy the positions of relatively high power or control. Such analytic comments can help to make processes more explicit, which in turn will lead to clearer feedback.

The degree to which a T-group will succeed in creating that climate which has an optimal mix of confirmation and disconfirmation is determined by many environmental factors. Thus some T-groups will be more successful in generating learning than others. Before entering into discussion of such factors, we need to examine studies of the overall effects of T-groups. Since T-groups represent a rather radical departure from more traditional training procedures, they have been criticized from a wide variety of viewpoints. Some critics see T-groups as a setting in which frustrated organization men can enjoy catharsis (Back, 1972; Rosenthal, 1971), thereby forestalling any pressure for change back on the job. Others acknowledge that T-groups will generate some pressure for change, but argue that such pressures will have little durability in conflict with the longer-term processes of control and social comparison in work organizations (Pugh, 1965). Thus changes should be found after T-group participation but they should be short-lived. Still other critics claim that T-groups are psychologically dangerous (Gottschalk and Pattison, 1969; Jaffe and Scherl, 1969). According to these critics, substantial numbers of T-group members are damaged by their experiences in groups.

Evaluation studies

A considerable number of follow-up studies of T-group trainees have been completed. These studies are reviewed by Campbell and Dunnette (1968) and by Cooper and Mangham (1971). Some of the most interesting studies are those using a procedure referred to as 'verified change'. In these studies trainees were contacted six to eight months after participating in a T-group and invited to complete an unstructured questionnaire on which they described whatever changes they had noted in their behaviour. In addition they provided a list of the names of those who worked closely with them. These people were then also asked to complete a questionnaire describing any changes in the trainee. The different reports on the same trainee were compared, through the use of a system of content analysis categories. Where two or more describers reported a change in the same category, this was considered as verified change. Bunker (1965) compared reports on 229 trainees with 112 control subjects, who had no training. He found one or more verified changes among sixty-seven per cent of the trainees but only thirty-three per cent of the controls. The changes found fell in eleven of the fifteen categories used, and included increased openness, receptivity and tolerance of differences; increased operational skill in interpersonal relationships; and improved understanding of self and others. Other verified change studies by Miles (1965) using elementary school principals, Boyd and Ellis (1962) using Canadian managers, Valiquet (1969) using United States managers, and Moscow (1971) using British and Dutch trainees have all yielded comparable differences between trainees and controls.

This type of evaluation study is vulnerable to a number of criticisms. The report writers may be biased in a number of ways. For example they may, unknown to the researcher, discuss their responses with one another; also they know who has been trained and who has not, which may make them likely to attribute changes to the trainees but not to the controls. Thirdly, the use of post-only measurements is a weakness. It may be that some people are in more change-prone settings, and that these are the people selected for training. Finally, the studies may show that behaviour change by the trainees occurs, but they do not test directly whether the changes are for the better or for the worse.

The studies by Boyd and Ellis and by Moscow compared the effects of T-group participation with the effects of other forms of training. These studies found T-groups to be more successful than the other forms of training, which considerably weakens the power of the first two criticisms, because these criticisms should apply equally to those who attended any kind of course. On balance the research findings are encouraging. It will in future be necessary to design more precise measures and to apply them before as well as after training. But at present the weight of evidence is that durable effects of the T-group do occur in a substantial proportion of trainees.

But what can be said as to whether the changes are either beneficial or harmful? The difficulty here is that it is rarely possible to provide an unambiguous criterion for the measure of the effectiveness of an individual within an organization. Underwood (1965) obtained ratings from colleagues as to whether changes arising from T-groups were for better or for worse. It turned out that where those in T-groups expressed themselves more forcefully on the job, this was judged to be a negative effect. More negative effects were found for trainees than controls. Clearly such a criterion of effectiveness is altogether too situation-bound. Plain speaking may have been detrimental, but equally it may have been just what was required even if organizational colleagues did not welcome it. The problem is not that T-groups have been shown to fail to increase an individual's effectiveness, but that measures of individual effectiveness have not been satisfactorily devised. This problem may be easier to resolve in studying the effects of T-groups on whole organizational units, since it is somewhat simpler to measure the effectiveness of units than of individuals. This will be considered in the next chapter.

The verified change studies referred to above give little encouragement to the hypothesis that T-groups damage people. The critics would probably respond by saying that in none of the verified change studies was anything like a one hundred per cent response rate achieved, and that those who are damaged are unlikely to return their forms. Batchelder and Hardy (1968) reviewed the experience of 1,200 Y.M.C.A. directors in T-groups. They followed up all instances of allegedly 'severe negative experiences'. They managed to find four such instances, but in only one of these had there not been a long-term beneficial outcome. Ross *et al.* (1971) contacted all psychiatrists in the Cincinatti area, requesting information on anyone on whom T-groups had had adverse effects. A number of such people were identified. This number was then compared with the number of those known to have attended groups in the Cincinatti area at the time. The proportion of those adversely affected turned out to be nineteen in 2,900, which is 0·7 per cent. This figure is likely to be not markedly higher than that for an equivalent population not attending T-groups.

What determines the success of training?

If T-groups have the potentiality of generating behaviour changes helpful to the trainee, then it is important to examine ways of making those effects more probable. Three ways in which this might be achieved are through variations in the way the group is composed, variations in the leader's behaviour, and variations in the time dimension. Taking first the question of composition, it is clear that a T-group composed of initial strangers will be markedly different from a T-group composed of a boss and his work subordinates. The first of these will find it a great deal easier to develop a climate of relationships where people speak freely, whereas in the second there will be stronger concerns about the long-term consequences of speaking out. In the development of T-group methods it was initially thought that the 'safety' of a stranger group was a prerequisite for the development of a sufficiently open T-group climate. T-groups were accordingly composed of participants from a wide variety of organizations and occupations. Such diversity inevitably emphasizes the 'confirmation' aspect of social comparisons within the T-group experience and reduces the 'disconfirmation' aspect. This is because the heterogeneous group will focus on those qualities or experiences which they do have in common. By contrast, the more occupationally homogeneous group have career rivalries, previous misunderstandings and task constraints more to the fore, which is likely to enhance the amount of disconfirmation they generate for one another.

It was suggested earlier that the ideal T-group would generate both confirmation and disconfirmation for its members. This implies that groups should be intermediate between homogeneity and heterogeneity. However, such a conclusion is not testable in such a simple form. This is because the level of confirmation and disconfirmation in groups is also subject to variation through differences in the leader's behaviour and the timing of the group. Unless these were held constant, valid tests of compositional effects would not be possible. The few existing studies of compositional effects (Pollack, 1971; Reddy, 1972) indicate that when groups are conducted among occupationally homogeneous populations the groups with the most heterogeneous personality mix do best.

However, the choice of T-group composition is most usually determined not so much by *how much* the participant will learn, as by the goals of training. Organizations have come to believe that learning which is organizationally relevant is more likely to arise in training programmes which are conducted within the organization than in heterogeneous programmes (Winn, 1966). Such reasoning is inherently plausible: if a trainee attends a heterogeneous training programme in which the bases of social comparison and processes of control are quite different from those in his own organization, he is likely to experience intergroup conflict on his return. His loyalty to his T-group will be pitted against the continuing culture of his work organization. Where such conflict arises, the most likely outcome is that the trainee makes use of what he has learned at the T-group in his relations with friends and family rather than within the work organization. As we shall see in the next chapter, organizations have attempted to resolve this problem by attempting to change not individuals, but whole organizations.

The potential influence of the leader on the outcome of the T-group is very great. T-groups have frequently been referred to as 'unstructured', in reference to the relative passivity of the leader. No greater misnomer could have been devised. There are perhaps three characteristic ways in which different leaders structure their groups at present. The most widely distributed leadership style derives from the influence of National Training Laboratories (N.T.L.) in the United States. Such a leader behaves in a relatively member-like manner. He shows the group how he wishes it to develop, by example. For instance, he expresses his feelings towards group members and encourages others to do likewise. A second style, which has been of some importance in Britain, is often linked with the Tavistock Institute and derives from the clinical model. The Tavistock leader holds himself aloof from his group. He may not reply when spoken to and sees his role as being to *interpret* what happens in the group. The third leader style has evolved most recently, and I shall refer to it as encounter leadership. The encounter leader directs his group by instruction. He makes extensive use of exercises, many of which are based on non-verbal exercises or the use of fantasy or role-playing. The distinctions between these three styles are not at all clear cut.

All the follow-up studies reported earlier were conducted with N.T.L.-type groups. Considering how long Tavistock groups have been in use, it is lamentable that no research studies into their possible differential effects were completed until recently. Harrow *et al.* (1971) found that Tavistock-type leadership did indeed create quite different group structure from N.T.L. leadership in a study in which each subject participated in one group of each kind. However, no measures were reported of the consequences of these differences in terms of type or amount of learning. A wide range of N.T.L. and encounter styles of leadership were compared by Lieberman *et al.* (1972). Marked differences in effects were found. The subjects were sixteen groups of students at Stanford. It was found that the most aggressive leaders had much higher rates of dropout from their groups, a lower proportion of favourable changes retained six months after training, and a higher proportion of casualties (Yalom *et al.*, 1971). The method of defining casualties used by these authors is open to question, but this does not affect the differences found between different leadership styles.

In terms of the confirmation–disconfirmation model, one would expect that the effective leader would vary his behaviour according to the setting. One might expect him to work for confirming experiences in disconfirming settings and for some disconfirming experiences in totally confirming settings. To some extent this can be seen to be happening as differing group leader styles evolve. For example, the relatively accepting N.T.L. leaders have been the ones to become most strongly involved in training within organizations. Encounter leaders have remained almost entirely outside organizations. Tavistock leaders have worked both within and outside organizations, but in this author's opinion their style of training is most suited to work outside the organization.

A number of researchers have proposed that identification with the leader is an important mechanism of T-group learning. Peters (1966) and Bolman (1971) both showed links between identification with the leader and change in the group. However, Cooper (1969) showed that identification with the leader did not successfully predict behaviour change on the job, subsequent to training, while whether or not the leader was seen as 'genuine' during the group did predict such change on the job. Much remains to be discovered as to the manner in which the leader affects T-group outcome.

The final variable affecting T-group outcome is that of time. The title of this chapter makes reference to the temporary nature of the T-group. Miles (1964) has argued that many temporary systems share properties deriving from their temporary nature. Thus, as well as T-groups, other residential training programmes, holidays, *ad hoc* working parties, shipboard journeys, committees and carnivals all share the properties of increased spontaneity, interpersonal risk-taking and more open expression of feelings. All of these settings overturn, in lesser or greater degree, the established bases of social comparison and control and thus generate some pressure for innovation.

Some of these temporary systems undoubtedly generate more long-term change than others. Part of this may be that some last longer than others. For example, Bunker and Knowles (1967) showed that T-groups spread over three weeks generated more verified change back on the job than did T-groups spread over two weeks. But a more important element is the degree of linkage between the temporary system and the permanent one. Training programmes and working parties within an organization do constitute temporary systems but they are none the less conducted within the context of the organization's values. Holidays and carnivals do not have this linkage to organizational values: indeed, their attractiveness is often the degree to which they are divorced from such values. In terms of a distinction made by Schein and Bennis (1965), training programmes and working parties will generate 'organizationally-relevant' learning, while holidays and carnivals will generate 'personally-relevant' learning. There is, of course, no reason why personally-relevant learning should be inapplicable within an organization. However, it is inherently more probable that changes arising out of organizationally-relevant programmes will be those which are compatible with the organization. For this reason, organizations have in some circumstances come to favour training programmes which seek to change their entire structure and climate. Participation by an individual in a T-group such as has been described in this chapter might be a component in such a scheme, particularly in the early phases of it. But from the organization's point of view the main significance of such an experience might be that it en-

TABLE 3 *Some attributes of different training methods in human relations*

Attribute	*T-groups*	*Other methods*
Leadership required of the trainer	Leader requires considerable training if he is to perform competently	Leadership skills are more readily acquired
Time dimension	A substantial period of time is required, preferably fairly continuous	Much easier to schedule in small units, or intermingled with one another
Conditions of participation	Will not succeed unless the participants are truly volunteers	Less vulnerable to low participant motivation
Probable consequences	(i) Increased interest in changing organizational procedures (ii) Preference for plain speaking rather than machiavellian procedures (iii) Cohesive bonds between those trained together, particularly if they are in contact subsequently	Any of these three consequences might arise out of the use of other methods, but they are less certain to do so

couraged the interest of the trainee in change and innovation. From the individual's point of view the significance might be considerably greater, as the research data reported have shown.

This chapter has been exclusively devoted to a single training method, which has been explored in some detail. There are plainly a variety of other methods by which one might seek to increase the skills of diagnosing organizational behaviour and of acting on one's diagnoses. For example, one might use case studies, role-playing or business games. Paradoxically, although some of these methods are used a good deal more widely than the T-group, they have been much less adequately researched (Smith, 1968). However, even in the absence of research data it is clear that one would use T-groups for training in somewhat different circumstances than one would use the other methods. Some of the properties of the different methods are compared in Table 3. Unless the conditions in the left-hand column of the table are met and the consequences are ones which are desired, methods other than T-groups are indicated.

We turn now to the difficult problem of applying the methods described in this chapter within organizations.

Summary

The application of increased understanding of groups and organizations necessitates the development of the individual's skills in relating to others. In T-groups this is attempted through the creation of a group in which participants examine and attempt to modify their own relationships. T-groups rely for their effect on intra-group social comparison and immunity from social control demands from other organizations.

Evaluation studies indicate that around two-thirds of trainees show lasting changes in their behaviour and there is little evidence of harmful effects. The successful T-group is one in which the participant's social comparisons generate for him a blend of confirmation and disconfirmation. The leader can enhance this blending through appropriate variations in group composition, time boundaries and his own behaviour.

The potency of long-term organizational pressures on the individual is such that training for individuals usually needs to be considered in a wider context of organizational planning for change.

VIII Changing Organizational Behaviour

Planned changes in organizational behaviour are by no means easy to achieve. The earlier chapters of this book have documented some of the many ways in which the behaviour of organization members is constrained or limited by others within the organization or by the environment within which the organization operates. To seek to change organizational behaviour is to attempt to break through some of these constraints. To be sure, advocates of organization change often argue that one should only attempt changes which are 'compatible' with the organization's readiness for change or the demands of its environment. But there are so many determinants of an organization's existing performance that *any* change is likely to be detrimental to someone or to some aspect of the organization.

Thus it need not be surprising that attempts at organization change quite often fail. Laboratory experiments also quite often fail to generate the predicted results. In one respect at least the student of organizational change is better off than the experimental social psychologist: a much higher proportion of failures achieve publication. The reason for this is not hard to divine. Within the laboratory experiment, the experimenter and the researcher are one and the same person. A researcher who frequently reports null findings lays himself open to criticisms – justified or not – this his experimental techniques are poor. On the other hand, the organizational change agent is at least sometimes not the same person as the researcher. The researcher who reports a failure to effect organizational change can do so without casting doubt on his own abilities. It is perhaps for this reason that the literature on organization change is well supplied with 'horror stories', which make all too clear some of the ways in which change should not be attempted.

Evaluation studies

Lest the reader conclude that all such change efforts are doomed to failure this chapter will begin with a relatively clearly delineated success story.

The Harwood manufacturing company in the United States has an extended history of deliberate attempts to apply social science approaches to the solution of their problems. In an earlier chapter the classic study by Coch and French (1948) which was conducted in their pyjama factory was discussed. In 1962 Harwood took over another pyjama firm, Weldon. The two organizations were in the same market and in many ways were similarly situated. However, Harwood was being participatively managed with considerable economic success, while Weldon's autocratic management were incurring heavy losses. Harwood decided to attempt to 'transplant' their organizational climate into Weldon. The story of this attempt is told by Marrow, Bowers and Seashore (1967). Between 1962 and 1964 an intensive change programme was under way, involving the use of engineering consultants, operator training, in-plant T-groups at senior levels, group discussion at more junior levels, union recognition, reorganization of work flow, and numerous other changes. Up to five different external change agents were in the organization at some times, although it had a total payroll of only 1,000. The researchers operated quite independently of the change agents.

This massive intervention led to dramatic changes in Weldon's performance. All changes were compared with the performance of the Harwood plant, which served as a control. In 1962, Weldon made a loss of fifteen per cent on capital invested, in contrast to Harwood's profit of seventeen per cent. By 1964 Weldon were achieving a profit of seventeen per cent in comparison to Harwood's twenty-one per cent. In the same period operator turnover fell from ten per cent per month to four per cent, while Harwood was steady at under one per cent; and absence rates fell from six per cent to three per cent with Harwood steady on three per cent.

The management system used by Harwood accords with Likert's participative model outlined earlier. Likert (1967) distinguishes four possible systems: (1) exploitative-authoritative; (2) benevolent-authoritative; (3) consultative; (4) participative-group. The fourth of these is the closest to practices which he advocates as most effective, and the first is most distant from these practices. Questionnaire measures assessing which of these styles were in operation at Weldon and Harwood, and also which styles would be preferred, were administered by the researchers. The Harwood figures confirmed that system 4 was dominant there. The organization moved farther in that direction during 1962/4. Weldon in 1962 was on the borderline between systems 1 and 2, whereas by 1964 they had achieved system 3.

The major organizational change programme concluded in 1964, but the researchers found that this change was still maintained in 1966. Indeed, Seashore and Bowers (1970) report a further follow-up study indicating some additional progress towards system 4 despite no further major training, and despite the fact that by 1969 considerable numbers of those involved in the actual change programme would no longer be at Weldon, on account of normal turnover.

Here then is an apparently successful attempt at introducing long-term major change in an organization. How was it achieved? Bowers and Seashore undertook a week by week analysis of production records in an attempt to identify which of the change programmes was most closely correlated with the marked upturn in productivity which occurred. They acknowledge the limitations of this procedure – it emphasizes short-run effects and would tend to ignore change efforts which have a longer-term effect. They concluded that four events were closely correlated with productivity increases:

Individualized training for those with below average production records;
T-groups for supervisors and staff;
sacking of a small number of very low producers;
discussion groups with shop-floor operatives.

This listing implies that the 'technological' changes, such as changes in work flow as well as changes in selection and initial training, were not important in achieving the effect. It was the more 'interpersonally-orientated' items which were most influential. However, Marrow *et al.* make the point that the technological innovations may have helped to create a climate where the interpersonal innovations were more acceptable.

A number of other researchers have found that the use of T-groups within organizations can lead to greater adoption of participative or system 4 management styles. For example, Golembiewski and Carrigan (1970a) used Likert's questionnaire with a group of sixteen sales managers. Changes from system 3 towards system 4 were found after training. Two further applications of the questionnaire showed that the changes persisted over at least eighteen months after training (Golembiewski and Carrigan,

1970b). In this instance there was no control group, so that one may be less confident that the changes were attributable to training rather than extraneous factors. Further accounts of programmes of organizational development relying heavily on the use of T-groups are provided by Beckhard (1966) and Davis (1967). In both cases no quantitative measurement is provided, nor is any kind of control or comparison group envisaged, but major changes in organizational functioning are claimed. Beckhard's work was with a hotel chain and Davis's was with a firm engaged in the space programme.

A programme which made some use of T-groups but which failed is carefully documented by Benedict *et al.* (1967). In this instance the target for change was a school system, 'South Stanton', in New Jersey. As in the Weldon study, a clear separation was maintained between the trainers and the researchers, although this was not always easy. Control data were obtained from a comparable school system in which no training was undertaken. The change intervention in this instance was undertaken in collaboration with the school system superintendent. A range of exploratory interviews were conducted leading to a four-day workshop attended by the superintendent and twenty-four other members of his system. This workshop did not produce much impetus for further activities and later measurements showed that little change had been achieved. If one contrasts this project with the Weldon project, there is an obvious difference in the type of organization concerned, but in the light of further examples to be explored shortly this seems unlikely to be the key difference. Two other differences were the scale of the project and the degree of commitment to it by senior management. For almost a year after the commencement of the Weldon project, little improvement was noted. None the less management had sufficient commitment to persist with the programme and ultimately more than recouped their losses. By contrast, at the first sign that the training would not produce quick improvement the school project was abandoned. At Weldon, the change project was initiated by management who went out and found the external resources they required. By contrast again, it was the change agents in the Benedict *et al.* study who approached the school superintendent, soliciting his involvement in their change project. Inevitably the superintendent was therefore a great deal less committed to the project than were Harwood management to their project.

A fascinating report by Schmuck *et al.* (1969) outlines an intervention in a junior high school named Highland Park in Portland, Oregon, which had more durable and beneficial consequences. The central component of training was a one-week programme for the entire staff of the school, shortly before the opening of the school year. The programme involved both T-groups and also exercises designed to facilitate the transfer of learning to the specific settings existing in the school. A number of further activities arose from this programme, involving continuing contacts with the external change agents. The following summer the school staff organized themselves a further training programme without outside assistance. Questionnaire measures indicate some lasting changes in the manner in which the school staff described their situation. In particular, they saw the behaviour of their principal in a much more favourable light, they evaluated the effectiveness of staff meetings much more favourably, they indicated a wide range of innovations during the year, and they showed increased openness and helpfulness to one another. Requests for transfers out of the school at the end of the year were three per cent compared to rates in other local schools of ten to sixteen per cent. The changes reported were all compared with similar measures derived from a number of control schools, none of whom showed similar changes. Schmuck *et al.* give very little detail of how the intervention was initiated. However, it is clear from their report that the principal was a key figure in its success. The change project was not something imposed on the school from outside but had very firm roots within the school. The report lacks any detail of the school's history which might clarify how such roots were established.

The focus of the Highland Park intervention was on a single school, in contrast to the South Stanton intervention, which spanned a group of schools comprising a school system. Neither paper gives very much demographic data, but it appears that the superintendent at South Stanton was at the time of the intervention under a good deal of conflicting pressure on the race issue. The Highland Park school in Portland was presumably not in this position. Rather than draw premature conclusions as to why one intervention succeeded where the other failed, let us first enlarge the sample of projects to be considered. One further carefully documented study of educational innovation is available. This concerns an attempt to introduce into a ghetto school in Boston ('Cambire') the kind of unstructured, discovery-orientated classroom methods which have been developed in Britain (Gross, Giacquinta and Bernstein, 1971). The school had less than 200 children and had been detached from the main school system in order to facilitate the introduction of change. It was responsible to the Bureau of Educational Change for the city. The staff were well disposed towards the introduction of change. Gross *et al.*'s data are based on observation, interviews and a small number of questionnaires. In contrast to all the organization change projects so far reviewed, no use was made of external change agents, nor were there any T-groups. Indeed, the only impetus for change was provided by two memoranda from the Director of the Bureau of Educational Change. These expounded the philosophy of the new approach proposed, but left it completely up to the teachers to work out ways of making them practicable. This change attempt was a complete failure: indeed, it changed a school of high morale to one of low morale. According to observation data collected after five months, one pair of teachers were using the new methods for forty per cent of the time, one pair for twenty-four per cent of the time, and none of the remaining pairs for more than thirteen per cent of the time.

Gross *et al.* conclude that for an innovation to succeed, five conditions must be met, none of which were at Cambire. Firstly, organization members must have a clear idea of what is the nature of the innovation proposed; secondly, they must have the requisite skills to implement it; thirdly, they must have the resources to carry it out; fourthly, other existing organizational procedures must be compatible rather than contradictory with the innovation; and fifthly, organization members must be willing to carry out the innovation. At Cambire, the failure to satisfy the first four conditions destroyed the initial willingness of the teachers to innovate. Perhaps the greatest failing of the innovators at Cambire was their apparent inability to see that their proposals imposed great pressures on the teachers to develop new skills, while at the same time giving them no opportunity to do so. Gross *et al.* express themselves cautiously about the widespread use of T-groups in organization change attempts, but the Cambire situation appears to be one in which their use would have been entirely justified. The skills the teachers needed would be quite similar to those which were successfully developed by the Highland Park project.

There are clearly situations in which the use of T-groups is inappropriate to the achievement of organizational change. Schein and Bennis (1965) report several case studies of such situations. These mostly hinge on the use of innovation procedures which are not sufficiently sanctioned by higher management. Training is carried out of which higher management is unaware. This is later discovered and brought to a halt with considerable ill-will on both sides. The potential consequences of this are well illustrated by the situation reported by Sykes (1962). The programme he studied did not involve T-groups but more orthodox human relations training for foremen. The programme led the foremen to the expectation that they would in future have a greater say within the company. When this turned out not to be so, more than half the trained foremen left in less than a year.

One attempt to link the effect of group training more closely into organizational change has been the 'managerial grid' programme developed by Blake and Mouton (1964). Essentially this argues that managers should be trained to place high but equal weight on the priorities of production and of interpersonal relations and that they should not make compromises when the two priorities are in conflict. According to this argument, acceptable problem solutions are those which satisfy both production and interpersonal criteria. Blake, Mouton, Barnes and Greiner (1964) report on evaluation of the application of this programme within a large oil company, 'Sigma'. Eight hundred managers were involved in one-week training programmes, and further training followed this in which workgroups spent time together working on the implications of their earlier training for their future work together. There was no control group in this study, but profits of several million dollars were attributed to the effects of training by the researchers. Marked changes in attitudes were also found. The scale of this intervention is reminiscent of the Weldon project and equally marked effects were found. However, in this instance it is less possible to be sure what caused these effects, since other major events occurred concurrently, such as the making redundant of 600 men.

A study of the effects of managerial grid training which did use a control group was that by Smith and Honour (1969). Some changes were found at the trained factory ('Alpha') which did not occur at the control factory ('Beta'). But these changes affected only a minority of trainees and were not so marked as those found by Blake *et al.* According to the Blake model the major benefits should have come at a later stage, but the management were lukewarm towards the project and did not persist with it. As with the South Stanton school system, their commitment was insufficient to sustain the effort in the face of initially discouraging results.

Friedlander (1970) claimed to have identified one determinant of the success or failure of T-groups within organizations. Reviewing the results of T-groups within a research and development station of the U.S. Army (Friedlander, 1967) he found that those groups with beneficial results already had high trust initially, while those which did less well had low initial trust. Trust itself did not change, but Friedlander claims that it mediated the other variables. This finding does not fit well with the results achieved at Weldon, where trust was initially extremely low. One might perhaps conclude that success is at any rate *easier* where trust is initially high. Greiner (1967a, b) has also attempted to delineate some factors separating successful organization change from the failures. At Sigma, he concluded that the history of the company over the previous thirty years and the prestige of Blake as a change agent both needed to be taken into account (1967a). More generally, he suggests that successful changes are often associated with some degree of external pressure on the organization, some internal tension or conflict; and the use of external as well as internal change agents. External pressure and internal conflict will both be likely to motivate the organization to seek solutions to its current problems. The use of external change agents means that, if they are well chosen, the organization has available specialist resources in facing up to these problems. Greiner's list is quite different from the preconditions for success proposed by Gross in analysing the failure of the Cambire school change project. Greiner's list is more global, while Gross's is more specific. The differences probably reflect the fields from which the authors drew their data. In industry, some firms at least have achieved considerable sophistication in introducing change. If a change effort fails it is less likely to be on account of the lack of the obvious prerequisites, such as information, resources and training, and more likely to be due to more complex factors. In education and the social services, on the other hand, the belief is still widespread that major changes may be achieved by decree. The Gross *et al.* study illustrates this, but many other cases are available.

One project which did attempt to provide the prerequisites for change and none the less failed was the Hospital Internal Communications Project in Britain (Wieland and Leigh, 1971; Revans, 1972). This attempted to improve communication procedures within ten hospitals in and around London. A change team was trained in each hospital. The training focused on the research methods of interviewing and questionnaire construction. Each team then made whatever investigations were appropriate within their hospital. A separate research team assessed the effects of the ten teams' investigations. Very little change was found. Some of the failings of this project appear to be that no clarity was achieved as to what changes were desired, effort was diffused over a wide field, and the training given was of questionable relevance. Such training assumes that once a problem has been identified by a suitable survey, it will solve itself. As with the Cambire situation, the implementation of change was weak.

In earlier chapters of this book, a good deal of emphasis was placed on the importance of the environment in determining social behaviour. It was suggested that each environment requires a particular form of corresponding organization. Most of the projects reviewed in this chapter have been to do with the use of participative group methods. There is considerable need for such methods in many settings, but if the earlier discussion is correct, there must be other settings in which changes away from participative procedures would be the required ones. One study confirming this likelihood is that of Taylor (1971). He assessed the effects of programmes attempting to move organizations towards Likert's system 4. In an insurance company the programme failed, while in a refinery it succeeded. Taylor analyses the refinery data and finds, as predicted, that the move towards system 4 was significantly stronger among those workgroups using complex technology.

In Chapter VI, some prominence was given to Lawrence and Lorsch's concepts of differentiation and integration of organization structure. Their approach implies that quite different types of organizational intervention would be required depending on whether it was necessary to increase or decrease, for example, differentiation. Lawrence and Lorsch (1969) report on a number of instances in which they attempted to achieve this. Their approach rests heavily on their diagnostic procedures. Using questionnaires and interviews, they arrive at figures for the actual and the desired state of organization's differentiation and integration. These findings are then shared with the management of the organization. Appropriate training is designed collaboratively. This may take the form of group discussion, case studies and so forth, but little detail is given of their procedures. Evaluation of this approach will need to wait on greater detail of the training and on published evaluations of the effects.

Some questions about values and about future developments

The studies reported in the present chapter and the previous one indicate that at least sometimes we do have the capacity to influence in fairly major ways the manner in which organizations and individuals behave. As time passes this expertise is likely to increase rather than decrease. This section is devoted to a consideration of ways in which this capacity should be used.

In this chapter, projects have been reported in which attempts were made to change schools, hospitals, manufacturing industry, insurance firms and a military organization. Space limitations prevented examination of similar, but less rigorously researched, attempts in prisons, mental hospitals, universities, the church and so forth. Writers on the process of organizational development have rather often described the process as though it were a technology applicable to any kind of organization whatever its goals. This model of the value-free 'technician', servicing the behavioural needs of organizations in order to enhance their efficiency, is a hard one to sustain. If one engages in an attempt to enhance the effectiveness of an organization, one is unquestionably implicated in the goals of that organization. The process of organization development may be neutral – the author has heard of its use not only among U.S. Army establishments but also with Maoist student groups in South America – but the change agent who works with a particular organization is far from neutral. His intervention is judged in the context of the organization's existing values and his involvement gives him some measure of responsibility for the organization's behaviour. This point is well illustrated by a recent study of Teahan (n.d.). Teahan evaluated the effect of T-groups and role-playing on black and white recruits to the Detroit police force. The training was focused around the race issue. It was found that relative to controls, the white trainees became *more* prejudiced and the black trainees less so. Teahan suggests that this occurred because the white officers saw the multiracial emphasis of training as confirming their fears that senior police were biased in favour of black recruits. Thus in this particular project a well-intentioned programme contributed to the strengthening of behaviour which it sought to reduce.

One of the reasons why value problems become more acute as one moves from individual training to organizational development is that the question of voluntarism becomes more salient. It is relatively easy for an individual to decline to attend a training programme; where a whole organization is involved, individual choice is much reduced. For example, in the Detroit police project and in the training done at Weldon, attendance was obligatory. Attempts to change behaviour through coercion have a long and not particularly distinguished history. The consequences of coercion depend a good deal on the interaction between the change goal and the change method. For instance, where the police attempted to coerce open-mindedness into their officers, an inconsistency was quickly apparent to the trainees. On the other hand, where the Weldon staff were strongly pressured into attending training, but the management showed their good intentions in other ways concurrently, the pressure was accepted. Thus there may be some ways which are *more effective* in inducing change coercively; but this provides no guidelines at all as to the permissible limits of coercion in inducing organization change. The level of coercion is most usually inherent in a particular organization; the point at which the change agent has real choice is the point at which he decides whether or not to work within a particular system. If he goes ahead his behaviour will from that point onward be interpreted within the mores of the organization in any event.

The studies discussed have indicated how change agents can create some measure of change within organizations. It should also be clear that such changes are by no means radical ones. In each case the organization subsequent to the change programme was recognizably similar in many ways to how it had been previously. Weldon was still engaged in manufacturing pyjamas and its management still had much more influence on the organization's culture than did workers. A question which will command increasing attention as our knowledge grows is whether such changes represent the maximum achievable change, or whether much more radically different forms of organization could be developed. Let us look at such possibilities first pessimistically and then optimistically.

The pessimistic position is perhaps the easier one to expound simply. In the course of this book we have seen the manner in which the processes of social comparison and social control determine the form of particular groups and organizations. To propose that radical innovations might be developed would be to suggest that these processes might somehow be held in abeyance. The breadth of circumstances in which they have been shown to obtain renders this somewhat implausible.

The optimistic position contradicts this. It argues instead that as this century advances it will become a matter of increasing urgency to invent new forms of organization in response to social change. The generalizations in this book arise out of studies conducted in groups and organizations as they are. It is essential to envisage such findings of social psychology not as timeless truths but as truths obtaining at a particular point in time. As circumstances change so may human needs, and this will both imply and permit organizational innovation. Two of the most potent social changes in our time are the increasing diffusion of relative affluence and higher educational levels. Whereas in 1900 it was relatively simple for a small group of men to maintain a tightly centralized control over a vast organization by virtue of their greatly superior knowledge and skills, this is becoming less true. Organizations now exist in which the majority of the employees are very highly educated. Such a change implies the possibility of much higher involvement and much less use of arbitrary control procedures. In the organizations of the future there may be less and less occasion for the exercise of direct control and more and more use of bargaining procedures based on social comparison processes.

Many people yearn for a state of affairs where the task in which a group or organization is engaged is attractive and involving and the 'interpersonal' factors of social comparison, control and exploitation do not exist. We saw in Chapter VII that such kinds of intense involvement can sometimes be created in temporary systems which are isolated from external control demands and that experiencing such involvement can be a beneficial experience. But much less can be said of the possibility of creating such involvement on a permanent basis. The future years are likely to entail increasing experimentation with 'self-directed' communities and organizations. The central problems that such organizations will need to confront are those of how to resolve questions of resource allocation and equity, where urgent external threats do not compel unity, where the use of arbitrary control is excluded and where the long-term nature of the interaction makes avoidance difficult.

Summary and review

Planned attempts at organizational change are by no means always successful. In the successful programme at Weldon, the changes appeared more closely related to the 'interpersonal' interventions than to the technological ones. More generally, change attempts succeed when their intention is clear, and when the requisite skills, resources, procedures and motivation are present. Successful programmes are often associated with a prior history of external pressure and internal tension, coupled with the use of both external and internal change agents.

Change agents do not operate in a value-free vacuum: they bear some responsibility for the effects they create. Their effectiveness in facilitating change to date has been shown to be substantial but not overwhelming. In the future there will be an increasing need to invent new forms of organization to accommodate the changes currently under way in our society.

In closing this book let us take a look at the relationship between the two somewhat separate segments of it. In the first six chapters the focus was on the way groups and organizations can be described and analysed, as they currently are. In contrast the remaining two chapters focused on newly developing methods of introducing change into groups and organizations. The distinguished social psychologist Kurt Lewin is credited with the remark that the best way to try to understand something is to try to change it. If this line of thinking is a valid one, then the material in the final two chapters should yield additional tests of the fruitfulness of the analytic framework developed earlier in the book. Are the successes and failures of T-groups and programmes of organizational development explicable in terms of the processes of social comparison and control?

The last two chapters suggest that successful change programmes are those that create novel bases of social comparison which are motivationally relevant to organization members. Where the members are not involved or where the opportunity to make comparisons is not available, the change efforts are abortive. The role of social control processes in such change is also important. The successful programmes appear to be those in which power figures approve the change efforts but do not attempt to prescribe the precise detail of how the change goals shall be achieved. Both change by decree and change in the face of obstruction from higher power figures are likely to be limited in their success.

It was argued in earlier chapters that the effects of social comparison and control were mediated by environmental factors such as the nature of the task and interrelations with other groups or organizations. This is nowhere more true than in the field of change. The failure of existing procedures to achieve goals creates a receptive climate for innovation, and the availability of practicable alternatives further enhances the possibilities. From these general comments one can construct a picture of an organization ripe for change and one which is not. An organization ripe for change would be one which was failing on some important goal and in which both power figures and others in the organization favoured an adaptive response; there would be available within the organization alternative sources of social comparison relevant to the causes of the failure and there would also be access to relevant resources from outside the organization, whether they be skills, alternative procedures, money, materials or new organization members. Conversely the organization not ripe for change will be relatively successful; power figures will not favour change; there will be no obvious alternative bases of social comparison and no access to external resources.

Clearly most groups and organizations fall somewhere between these two extremes. Continuing developments in influencing the levels of change and stability in groups and organizations will rest on our obtaining more precise understanding of which of these various dimensions are most important under what circumstances. For the present we have a set of concepts and procedures which are of some use in guiding our actions.

References

Adams, J. S., 'Inequity in social exchange'. In L. Berkowitz (ed.), *Advances in experimental social psychology*, vol. 2. New York: Academic Press, 1965, pp. 267–99

Adams, J. S., and Jacobsen, P. R., 'Effects of wage inequities on work quality'. *Journal of Abnormal and Social Psychology*, 1964, *69*, 19–25

Adams, J. S., and Rosenbaum, W. E., 'The relationship of worker productivity to cognitive dissonance about wage inequities'. *Journal of Applied Psychology*, 1962, *46*, 161–4

Allport, F. H., 'The influence of the group upon association and thought'. *Journal of Experimental Psychology*, 1920, *3*, 159–82

Andrews, I. R., 'Wage inequity and job performance'. *Journal of Applied Psychology*, 1967, *51*, 39–45

Argyris, C., 'Some unintended consequences of rigorous research'. *Psychological Bulletin*, 1968, *70*, 185–97

Argyris, C., 'The incompleteness of social–psychological theory'. *American Psychologist*, 1969, *24*, 893–908

Aronson, E., 'The theory of cognitive dissonance: a current perspective'. In L. Berkowitz (ed.), *Advances in experimental social psychology*, vol. 4. New York: Academic Press, 1969, pp. 1–34

Asch, S. E., 'Studies of independence and conformity: a minority of one against a unanimous majority'. *Psychological Monographs*, 1956, *70*, no. 9 (Whole No. 416)

Back, K. W., *Beyond Words: the story of sensitivity training and the encounter movement*. New York: Russell Sage Foundation, 1972

Bales, R. F., 'Task roles and social roles in problem-solving groups'. In E. E. Maccoby, T. M. Newcomb and R. L. Hartley (eds), *Readings in social psychology*. New York: Holt, 1958; third edition, pp. 437–46

Barker, R. G., and Gump, P. V., *Big school, small school: high school size and student behaviour*. Stanford: Stanford U.P., 1964

Barker, R. G., *Ecological psychology: concepts and methods for studying the environment of human behaviour*. Stanford: Stanford U.P., 1968

Batchelder, R. L., and Hardy, J. M., *Using sensitivity training and the laboratory method: an organisational case study in the development of human resources*. New York: Association Press, 1968

Baumrind, D., 'Some thoughts on ethics of research: on reading Milgram's "Behavioural study of obedience"'. *American Psychologist*, 1964, *19*, 421–3

Bavelas, A., 'A mathematical model for group structures'. *Applied Anthropology*, 1948, *7*, 16–30

Beckhard, R., 'An organisation improvement programme in a decentralised organisation'. *Journal of Applied Behavioural Science*, 1966, *2*, 3–26

Benedict, B. A., Calder, P. H., Callahan, D. M., Hornstein, H. A., and Miles, M. B., 'The clinical–experimental approach to assessing organisational change efforts'. *Journal of Applied Behavioural Science*, 1967, *3*, 347–80

Benne, K. D., 'History of the T-group in the laboratory setting'. In L. P. Bradford, J. R. Gibb and K. D. Benne (eds), *T-group theory and laboratory method: innovation in re-education*. New York: Wiley, 1964, pp. 80–135

Bennett, E. B., 'Discussion, decision, commitment and consensus in "group decision" '. *Human Relations*, 1955, *8*, 251–74

Blake, R. R. and Mouton, J. S., 'The intergroup dynamics of win–lose conflict and problem-solving collaboration in union-management relations'. In M. Sherif (ed.), *Intergroup relations and leadership: approaches and research in industrial, ethnic, cultural and political areas*. New York: Wiley, 1962, pp. 94–141

Blake, R. R., and Mouton, J. S., *The managerial grid*. Houston: Gulf Publishing, 1964

Blake, R. R., and Mouton, J. S., 'The union–management intergroup laboratory'. *Journal of Applied Behavioural Science*, 1965, *1*, 25–57

Blake, R. R., Mouton, J. S., Barnes, L. B., and Greiner, L., 'Breakthrough in organisational development'. *Harvard Business Review*, 1964, *42*, 133–55

Bolman, L., 'Some effects of trainers on their T-groups'. *Journal of Applied Behavioural Science*, 1971, *7*, 309–25

Bouchard, T. J., Jr, 'Personality, problem-solving procedure and performance in small groups'. *Journal of Applied Psychology Monographs*, 1969, *53*, 1–29

Boyd, J. B., and Elliss, J. D., *Findings of research into senior management seminars*. Toronto: Hydro-electric power commission of Ontario, 1962

Brown, R., *Social Psychology*. New York: Free Press, 1965

Bunker, D. R., 'Individual applications of laboratory training'. *Journal of Applied Behavioural Science*, 1965, *1*, 131–47

Bunker, D. R., and Knowles, E. S., 'Comparison of behavioural changes resulting from human relations training laboratories of different lengths'. *Journal of Applied Behavioural Science*, 1967, *3*, 505–23

Campbell, J. P., and Dunnette, M. D., 'Effectiveness of T-group experiences in managerial training and development'. *Psychological Bulletin*, 1968, *70*, 73–104

Caplow, T., *Two against one: coalitions in triads*. Englewood Cliffs, N.J.: Prentice-Hall, 1968

Carey, A., 'The Hawthorne studies: a radical critique'. *American Sociological Review*, 1967, *32*, 403–16

Carlson, S., *Executive behaviour: a study of the workload and working methods of managing directors*. Stockholm: Stromberg, 1951

Christie, R., and Geis, F. L. (eds), *Studies in machiavellianism*. New York: Academic Press, 1970

Christie, R., Gergen, K. J., and Marlowe, D., 'The penny-dollar caper'. In R. Christie and F. L. Geis (eds), *Studies in Machiavellianism*. New York: Academic Press, 1970, pp. 173–89

Clark, R. D., III, 'Group induced shift toward risk: a critical appraisal'. *Psychological Bulletin*, 1971, *76*, 251–71

Coch, L., and French, J. R. P., Jr, 'Overcoming resistance to change'. *Human Relations*, 1948, *1*, 512–32

Collins, B. E., and Guetzkow, H., *A social psychology of group processes for decision-making*. New York: Wiley, 1964

Collins, O., Dalton, M., and Roy, D., 'Restriction of output and social cleavage in industry'. *Applied Anthropology*, 1946, *5*, 1–14

Cooper, C. L., 'The influence of the trainer on participant change in T-groups'. *Human Relations*, 1969, *22*, 515–30

Cooper, C. L., and Mangham, I. L., *T-groups: a survey of research*. London: Wiley, 1971

Crutchfield, R. S., 'Conformity and character'. *American Psychologist*, 1955, *10*, 191–8

Dalton, M., *Men who manage*. New York: Wiley, 1959

Danziger, K., *Socialisation*. Harmondsworth: Penguin, 1971

Darley, J. M., and Aronson, E., 'Self-evaluation vs. direct anxiety reduction as determinants of the fear-affiliation relationship'. *Journal of Experimental Social Psychology*, 1966, suppl. *1*, 66–79

Davis, J. H., *Group performance*. Reading, Mass.: Addison-Wesley, 1969

Davis, S., 'An organic problem-solving method of organisation change'. *Journal of Applied Behavioural Science*, 1967, *3*, 3–21

Deutsch, M., Epstein, Y., Canavan, D., and Gumpert, P., 'Strategies of inducing cooperation: an experimental study'. *Journal of Conflict Resolution*, 1967, *11*, 345–60

Deutsch, M., and Solomon, L., 'Reactions to evaluations by others as influenced by self-evaluations'. *Sociometry*, 1959, *22*, 93–112

Dion, K. L., Baron, R. S., and Miller, N., 'Why do groups make riskier decisions than individuals?' In L. Berkowitz (ed.), *Advances in experimental social psychology*, vol. 5. New York: Academic Press, 1970, pp. 305–77

Exline, R., Thibaut, J., Hickey, C. B., and Gumpert, P., 'Visual interaction in relation to machiavellianism and an unethical act'. In R. Christie and F. L. Geis (eds), *Studies in machiavellianism*. New York: Academic Press, 1970, pp. 53–76

Festinger, L., 'A theory of social comparison processes'. *Human Relations*, 1954, *7*, 117–40

Festinger, L., *A theory of cognitive dissonance*. Evanston, Ill.: Row, Peterson, 1957

Festinger, L., Schachter, S., and Back, K., *Social pressures in informal groups: a study of human factors in housing*. New York: Harper, 1950

Fiedler, F. E., *A theory of leadership effectiveness*. New York: McGraw Hill, 1967

Fiedler, F. E., 'Validation and extension of the contingency model of leadership effectiveness: a review of empirical findings'. *Psychological Bulletin*, 1971(a), *76*, 128–48

Fiedler, F. E., 'Note on the methodology of the Graen, Alvares & Orris studies testing the contingency model'. *Journal of Applied Psychology*, 1971(b) *55*, 202–4

Fiedler, F. E., 'Personality, motivational systems and the behaviour of high and low LPC persons'. *Human Relations*, 1972, *25*, 391–412

Fiedler, F. E., O'Brien, G. E., and Ilgen, D. R., 'The effect of leadership style upon the performance and adjustment of volunteer teams operating in a stressful foreign environment'. *Human Relations*, 1969, *22*, 503–14

Fleishman, E. A., and Harris, E. F., 'Patterns of leadership behaviour related to employee grievances and turnover'. *Personnel Psychology*, 1962, *15*, 43–56

French, J. R. P., Jr, Israel, J., and Ås, D., 'An experiment on participation in a Norwegian factory'. *Human Relations*, 1960, *13*, 3–19

Friedlander, F., 'The impact of organisational training laboratories upon the effectiveness and interaction of ongoing work groups'. *Personnel Psychology*, 1967, *20*, 289–309

Friedlander, F., 'The primacy of trust as a facilitator of further group accomplishment'. *Journal of Applied Behavioural Science*, 1970, *6*, 387–400

Friedman, A., and Goodman, P., 'Wage inequity, self-qualifications and productivity'. *Organizational Behaviour and Human Performance*, 1967, *2*, 406–17

Geis, F., Weinheimer, S., and Berger, D., 'Playing legislature: cool heads and hot issues'. In R. Christie and F. L. Geis (eds), *Studies in machiavellianism*. New York: Academic Press, 1970, pp. 190–209

Gergen, K. J., *The psychology of behaviour exchange*. Reading, Mass.: Addison-Wesley, 1969

Goldthorpe, J. H., Lockwood, D., Bechhofer, F., and Platt, J., *The affluent worker: industrial attitudes and behaviour*. Cambridge: Cambridge University Press, 1968

Golembiewski, R. T., *The small group: an analysis of research concepts and operations*. Chicago: University of Chicago Press, 1962

Golembiewski, R. T., and Carrigan, S. B., 'Planned change in organisation style based on the laboratory approach'. *Administrative Science Quarterly*, 1970a, *15*, 79–93

Golembiewski, R. T., and Carrigan, S. B., 'The persistence of laboratory-induced changes in organisation styles'. *Administrative Science Quarterly*, 1970b, *15*, 330–40

Goodman, P. S., and Friedman, A., 'An examination of Adams' theory of inequity'. *Administrative Science Quarterly*, 1971, *16*, 271–88

Gottschalk, L. A., and Pattison, E. M., 'Psychiatric perspectives on T-groups and the laboratory movement: an overview'. *American Journal of Psychiatry*, 1969, *126*, 823–39

Graen, G. B., Alvares, K., Orris, J. B., and Martella, J. A., 'Contingency model of leadership effectiveness: antecedent and evidential results'. *Psychological Bulletin*, 1970, *74*, 183–94

Graen, G. B., Alvares, K., and Orris, J. B., 'Contingency model of leadership effectiveness: some experimental results'. *Journal of Applied Psychology*, 1971, *55*, 196–201

Greiner, L. E., 'Antecedents of planned organisation change'. *Journal of Applied Behavioural Science*, 1967a, *3*, 51–85

Greiner, L. E., 'Patterns of successful organisation change'. *Harvard Business Review*, 1967b, *45*, 119–28

Gross, N., Giacquinta, J. B., and Bernstein, M., *Implementing organisational innovations: a sociological analysis of planned educational change.* New York: Harper, Row, 1971

Gross, N., Mason, W. S., and McEachern, A. W., *Explorations in role analysis: studies in the school superintendency role.* New York: Wiley, 1958

Hakmiller, K. L., 'Threat as a determinant of downward comparison'. *Journal of Experimental Social Psychology*, 1966, suppl. *1*, 32–9

Harford, T., and Solomon, L., 'Effects of a "reformed sinner" and a "lapsed saint" strategy upon trust formation in paranoid and non-paranoid schizophrenic patients'. *Journal of Abnormal Psychology*, 1969, *74*, 498–504

Hargreaves, D., *Social relations in a secondary modern school.* London: Routledge, Kegan Paul, 1967

Harrow, M., Astrachan, B. M., Tucker, G. J., Klein, E. B., and Miller, J. C., 'The T-group and study group laboratory experiences'. *Journal of Social Psychology*, 1971, *85*, 225–37

Hearn, G., 'Leadership and the spatial factor in small groups'. *Journal of Abnormal and Social Psychology*, 1957, *54*, 269–73

Heider, F., *The psychology of interpersonal relations.* New York: Wiley, 1958

Helmreich, R. L., and Collins, B. E., 'Situational determinants of affiliative preference under stress'. *Journal of Personality and Social Psychology*, 1967, *6*, 79–85

Hollander, E. P., 'Competence and conformity in the acceptance of influence'. *Journal of Abnormal and Social Psychology*, 1960, *61*, 365–9

Hollander, E. P., and Julian, J. W., 'Studies in leader legitimacy, influence and innovation'. In L. Berkowitz (ed.), *Advances in Experimental Social Psychology*, vol. 5. New York: Academic Press, 1970, pp. 33–69

Hollander, E. P., and Willis, R. H., 'Some current issues in the psychology of conformity and non-conformity'. *Psychological Bulletin*, 1967, *68*, 62–76

Homans, G. C., *The Human Group.* New York: Harcourt, Brace and World, 1950

Homans, G. C., *Social Behaviour: its elementary forms.* New York: Harcourt, Brace and World, 1961

Homans, G. C., *The nature of social science.* New York: Harcourt, Brace and World, 1967

Horne, J. H., and Lupton, T., 'The work activities of "middle" managers'. *Journal of Management Studies*, 1965, *1*, 14–33

Hovland, C. I., 'Reconciling conflicting results derived from experimental and survey studies of attitude change'. *American Psychologist*, 1959, *14*, 8–17

Hulin, C. L., and Blood, M. R., 'Job enlargement, individual differences and worker responses'. *Psychological Bulletin*, 1968, *69*, 41–55

Jaffé, S. L., and Scherl, D. J., 'Acute psychosis precipitated by T-group experiences'. *Archives of General Psychiatry*, 1969, *21*, 443–8

Kahn, R. L., Wolfe, D. M., Quinn, R. P., Snoek, J. D., and Rosenthal, R. A., *Organisational stress: studies in role conflict and ambiguity.* New York: Wiley, 1964

Kelman, H. C., *A time to speak: on human values and social research.* San Francisco: Jossey-Bass, 1968

Kogan, N., and Wallach, M. A., 'Risk-taking as a function of the situation, the person and the group'. In T. M. Newcomb (ed.), *New Directions in Psychology III.* New York: Holt, Rinehart and Winston, 1967

Lacey, C., *Hightown Grammar: the school as a social system.* Manchester: Manchester University Press, 1970

Lawrence, P. R., and Lorsch, J. W., *Organisation and environment: managing differentiation and integration.* Division of research, Graduate School of Business, Harvard University, 1967

Lawrence, P. R., and Lorsch, J. W., *Developing organisations: diagnosis and action.* Reading, Mass.: Addison-Wesley, 1969

Leavitt, H. J., 'Some effects of certain communication patterns on group performance'. *Journal of Abnormal and Social Psychology*, 1951, *46*, 38–50

Lewin, K., 'Group decision and social change'. In E. E. Maccoby, T. M. Newcomb and R. L. Hartley (eds), *Readings in social psychology.* 3rd edition. New York: Holt, 1958, pp. 197–211

Lieberman, M. A., Yalom, I. D., and Miles, M. B., 'The impact of encounter groups on participants: some preliminary findings'. *Journal of Applied Behavioural Science* 1972, *8*, 29–50

Likert, R., *New Patterns of management.* New York: McGraw Hill, 1961

Likert, R., *The human organisation: its management and values.* New York: McGraw Hill, 1967

Lippitt, R., and White, R. K., 'An experimental study of leadership and group life'. In E. E. Maccoby, T. M. Newcomb and R. L. Hartley (eds), *Readings in social psychology.* 3rd edition. New York: Holt, 1958, pp. 496–510

Lowin, A., 'Participative decision-making: a model, literature critique and prescriptions for research'. *Organizational Behaviour and Human Performance*, 1968, *3*, 68–106

Lowin, A., and Craig, J. R., 'The influence of level of performance on managerial style: an experimental object lesson in the ambiguity of correlational data'. *Organizational Behaviour and Human Performance*, 1968, *3*, 440–58

Lupton, T., *On the shop floor.* Oxford: Pergamon, 1963

Madaras, G. R., and Bem, D. J., 'Risk and conservatism in group decision-making'. *Journal of Experimental Social Psychology*, 1968, *4*, 350–65

Maier, N. R. F., and Hoffman, L. R., 'Using trained "developmental" discussion leaders to improve further the quality of group decisions'. *Journal of Applied Psychology*, 1960, *44*, 247–51

Mann, R. D., 'A review of the relationships between personality and performance in small groups'. *Psychological Bulletin*, 1959, *56*, 241–70

Marquis, D. G., 'Individual responsibility and group decisions involving risk'. *Industrial Management Review*, 1962, *3*, 8–23

Marrow, A. J., Bowers, D. G., and Seashore, S. E., *Management by participation: creating a climate for personal and organisational development.* New York: Harper, Row, 1967

Miles, M. B., 'On temporary systems'. In M. B. Miles (ed.), *Innovation in education.* New York: Bureau of Publications, Teachers College, Columbia University, 1964, pp. 437–90

Miles, M. B., 'Changes during and following laboratory training: a clinical–experimental study'. *Journal of Applied Behavioural Science*, 1965, *1*, 215–42

Milgram, S., 'Behavioural study of obedience'. *Journal of Abnormal and Social Psychology*, 1963, *67*, 371–8

Milgram, S., 'Issues in the study of obedience: reply to Baumrind'. *American Psychologist*, 1964(a), *19*, 848–52

Milgram, S., 'Group pressures and action against a person'. *Journal of Abnormal and Social Psychology*, 1964 (b), *69*, 137–43

Milgram, S., 'Liberating effects of group pressures'. *Journal of Personality and Social Psychology*, 1965(a), *1*, 127–34

Milgram, S., 'Some conditions of obedience and disobedience to authority'. *Human Relations*, 1965(b), *18*, 57–76

Morse, N. C., and Reimer, E., 'The experimental change of a major organisational variable'. *Journal of Abnormal and Social Psychology*, 1956, *52*, 120–29

Moscow, D., 'T-group training in the Netherlands: an evaluation and cross-cultural comparison'. *Journal of Applied Behavioural Science*, 1971, *7*, 427–48

Nemeth, C., 'Bargaining and reciprocity'. *Psychological Bulletin*, 1970, *74*, 297–308

Newcomb, T., *Personality and social change: attitude formation in a student community*. New York: Holt, Rinehart and Winston, 1943

Newcomb, T., *The acquaintance process*. New York: Holt, Rinehart and Winston, 1961

Olson, P., and Davis, J. H., 'Divisible tasks and pooling performance in groups'. *Psychological Reports*, 1964, *15*, 511–17

Osborn, A. F., *Applied imagination*. New York: Scribner's, 1957

Patchen, M. *The choice of wage comparisons*. Englewood Cliffs, N.J.: Prentice-Hall, 1961(a)

Patchen, M., 'A conceptual framework and some empirical data regarding comparisons of social rewards'. *Sociometry*, 1961(b), *24*, 136–56

Pelz, D. C., and Andrews, F. M., *Scientists in organisations: productive climates for research and development*. New York: Wiley, 1966

Peters, D. R., *Identification and personal change in laboratory training*. Unpublished doctoral dissertation, School of Industrial Management, M.I.T., 1966

Pollack, H. B., 'Change in homogeneous and heterogeneous sensitivity training groups'. *Journal of Consulting and Clinical Psychology*, 1971, *37*, 60–66

Pritchard, R. D., 'Equity theory: a review'. *Organizational Behaviour and Human Performance*, 1969, *4*, 176–211

Pugh, D. S., 'T-group training from the point of view of organisational theory'. In F. P. G. Whitaker (ed.), *T-group training: group dynamics in management education*. Oxford: Blackwell, 1965, pp. 44–50

Radloff, R., and Helmreich, R. L., *Groups under stress: psychological research in Sealab II*. New York: Appleton, Century-Crofts, 1968

Raven, B. H., and French, J. R. P., Jr, 'Legitimate power, coercive power and observability in social influence'. *Sociometry*, 1958, *21*, 83–97

Reddy, W. B., 'Interpersonal compatibility and self-actualisation in sensitivity training'. *Journal of Applied Behavioural Science*, 1972, *8*, 237–40

Revans, R. W., *Hospitals: communication, choice and change*. London: Tavistock, 1972

Roethlisberger, F. J., and Dickson, W. J., *Management and the worker*. Cambridge, Mass.: Harvard University Press, 1939

Rosenthal, B. G., 'The nature and development of the encounter group movement'. In L. Blank, G. B. Gottsegen and M. G. Gottsegen (eds), *Confrontation: encounters in self and interpersonal awareness*. New York: MacMillan, 1971

Rosenthal, R., and Rosnow, R. L. (eds), *Artifact in behavioural research*. New York: Academic Press, 1969

Ross, W. D., Kligfeld, M., and Whitman, R. W., 'Psychiatrists, patients and sensitivity groups'. *Archives of General Psychiatry*, 1971, *25*, 178–80

Sayles, L. R., *The behaviour of industrial work groups*. New York: Wiley, 1958

Schachter, S., *The psychology of affiliation: experimental studies of the sources of gregariousness*. Stanford, Calif.: Stanford University Press, 1959

Schein, E. H., and Bennis, W. G., *Personal and organisational change through group methods: the laboratory approach*. New York: Wiley, 1965

Schmuck, R. A., Runkel, P. J., and Langmeyer, D., 'Improving organisational problem-solving in a school faculty'. *Journal of Applied Behavioural Science*, 1969, *5*, 455–82

Schultz, D. P., *Panic behaviour*. New York: Random House, 1964

Seashore, S. E., *Group cohesiveness in the industrial work group*. Ann Arbor. Mich.: Institute for Social Research, 1954

Seashore, S. E., and Bowers, D. G., 'Durability of organisational change', *American Psychologist*, 1970, *25*, 227–33

Shaw, M. E., 'Communication networks.' In L. Berkowitz (ed.), *Advances in experimental social psychology*, vol. 1. New York: Academic Press, 1964, pp. 111–47

Shaw, M. E., and Blum, J. M., 'Effects of leadership style upon group performance as a function of task structure'. *Journal of Personality and Social Psychology*, 1966, *3*, 238–42

Sherif, M., *The psychology of social norms*. New York: Harper, 1936

Sherif, M., *Group conflict and co-operation: their social psychology*. London: Routledge, Kegan Paul, 1967

Slater, P. E., 'Role differentiation in small groups'. *American Sociological Review*, 1955, *20*, 300–310

Smith, P. B., 'Differentiation between sociometric rankings: a test of four theories'. *Human Relations*, 1963, *16*, 335–50

Smith, P. B., 'Training and developing executives'. In D. Pym (ed.), *Industrial Society: social sciences in management*. Harmondsworth: Penguin, 1968

Smith, P. B., and Honour, T. F., 'The impact of phase I managerial grid training'. *Journal of Management Studies*, 1969, *6*, 318–30

Snadowsky, A., 'Communication-network research: an examination of controversies'. *Human Relations*, 1972, *25*, 283–306

Sommer, R., 'Small group ecology'. *Psychological Bulletin*, 1967, *67*, 145–52

Sommer, R., *Personal space: the behavioural basis of design*. Englewood Cliffs, N.J.: Prentice-Hall, 1969

Steinzor, B., 'The spatial factor in face to face discussion groups'. *Journal of Abnormal and Social Psychology*, 1950, *45*, 552–5

Stoner, J. F., *A comparison of individual and group decisions including risk*. Unpublished master's thesis, School of Industrial Management, M.I.T., 1961

Stouffer, S. A., Suchman, E. A., Devinney, L. C., Star, S. A., and Williams, R. N., *The American soldier:* vol.1, *Adjustment during army life*. Princeton, N.J.: Princeton University Press, 1949

Strauss, G., 'Notes on power equalisation'. In H. J. Leavitt (ed.), *The Social science of organizations: four perspectives*. Englewood Cliffs, N.J.: Prentice-Hall, 1963, pp. 39–84

Swinth, R. L., 'The establishment of the trust relationship'. *Journal of Conflict Resolution*, 1967, *11*, 335–44

Sykes, A. J. M., 'The effects of a supervisory training course in changing supervisors' perceptions and expectations of the role of management'. *Human Relations*, 1962, *15*, 227–44

Taylor, D., Berry, P. C., and Block, C. H., 'Does group participation when using brainstorming facilitate or inhibit creative thinking?' *Administrative Science Quarterly*, 1958, *3*, 23–47

Taylor, J. C., 'Some effects of technology in organisation change'. *Human Relations*, 1971, *24*, 105–23

Teahan, J. E., *Role playing and group experience to facilitate intragroup dialogue*. Mimeographed, Wayne State University, Detroit, no date.

Thibaut, J. W., 'The development of contractual norms in bargaining: replication and variation'. *Journal of Conflict Resolution*, 1968, *12*, 102–12

Thibaut, J. W., and Kelley, H. H., *The social psychology of groups*. New York: Wiley, 1959

Thornton, D. A., and Arrowood, A. J., 'Self-evaluation, self-enhancement and the locus of social comparison'. *Journal of Experimental Social Psychology*, 1966, Suppl. *1*, 40–48

Triplett, N., 'The dynamogenic factors in pacemaking and competition'. *American Journal of Psychology*, 1898, 9, 507–33

Trist, E. L., Higgin, G., Pollock, H. E., and Murray, H. A., *Organisational choice*. London: Tavistock, 1963

Underwood, W. J., 'Evaluation of laboratory method training'. *Training Directors' Journal*, 1956, *19*, 34–40

Valiquet, M. I., 'Individual change in a management development programme'. *Journal of Applied Behavioural Science*, 1968, *4*, 313–26

Verba, S., *Small groups and political behaviour: a study of leadership*. Princeton, N.J.: Princeton University Press, 1961

Vroom, V., *Some personality determinants of the effects of participation*. Englewood Cliffs, N.J.: Prentice-Hall, 1960

Wallach, M. A., and Wing, C. W., Jr., 'Is risk a value?' *Journal of Personality and Social Psychology*, 1968, *9*, 101–6

Wallston, K. A., 'Performance styles as a determinant of effectiveness in an information-seeking task'. *Journal of Personality*, 1972, *40*, 211–25

Walton, R. E., *Interpersonal peacemaking: confrontations and third-party consultation*. Reading,Mass.: Addison-Wesley, 1969

Weick, K. E., 'Organisations in the laboratory'. In V. Vroom (ed.), *Methods of organisational research*. Pittsburgh: University of Pittsburgh Press, 1967, pp. 1–56

Weiss, W., 'Effects of the mass media of communication'. In G. Lindzey and E. Aronson (eds), *Handbook of social psychology*, pp. 77–195, vol. 5 (2nd edition). Reading, Mass.: Addison-Wesley, 1969

Wheeler, L., 'Motivation as a determinant of upward comparison'. *Journal of Experimental Social Psychology*, 1966, Suppl. *1*, 27–31

Wheeler, L., *et al.*, 'Factors determining choice of a comparison other'. *Journal of Experimental Social Psychology*, 1969, 5, 219–32

Wieland, G. F., and Leigh, H. (eds), *Changing hospitals: a report on the hospital internal communications project*. London: Tavistock, 1971

Willis, R. H. and Hollander, E. P., 'An experimental study of three response modes in social influence situations'. *Journal of Abnormal and Social Psychology*, 1964, *69*, 150–56

Winn, A., 'Social change in industry: from insight to implementation'. *Journal of Applied Behavioural Science*, 1966, *2*, 170–84

Woodward, J., *Industrial organisation: theory and practice*. London: Oxford University Press, 1965

Wrightsman, L. S., Jr, 'Effects of waiting with others on changes in level of felt anxiety'. *Journal of Abnormal and Social Psychology*, 1960, *61*, 216–22

Yalom, I., and Lieberman, M. A., 'A study of encounter group casualties'. *Archives of General Psychiatry*, 1971, *25*, 16–30

Zajonc, R., 'Social facilitation'. *Science*, 1965, *149*, 269–74

Zald, M., 'Power balance and staff conflict in correctional institutions'. *Administrative Science Quarterly*, 1962, *7*, 22–49

Index